Guests
of the
Emperor

Guests
of the
Emperor

The Secret History of
Japan's Mukden POW Camp

LINDA GOETZ HOLMES

NAVAL INSTITUTE PRESS
Annapolis, Maryland

Naval Institute Press
291 Wood Road
Annapolis, MD 21402

Library of Congress Cataloging-in-Publication Data
Holmes, Linda Goetz.
 Guests of the emperor / Linda Goetz Holmes.
    p. cm.
 Includes bibliographical references and index.
 ISBN 978-1-59114-377-2 (alk. paper)
 1. Mukden (Prisoner of war camp) 2. World War, 1939-1945—Prisoners
and prisons, Japanese. 3. World War, 1939-1945—Conscript labor—Japan.
4. Prisoners of war—Japan. 5. Prisoners of war—United States. 6.
Mitsubishi Zaibatsu—History. 7. Shenyang (Liaoning Sheng, China)—
History, Military—20th century. I. Title.
 DS805.J3H65 2010
 940.54'7252095181--dc22
                        2010009803

Printed in the United States of America on acid-free paper

17 16 15 14 13 12 11 10   9 8 7 6 5 4 3 2
First printing

Contents

Illustrations

Acknowledgments

Over the past fifteen years, as I gathered data on this most mysterious of Japanese prisoner-of-war camps, many, many people have helped me in my work. Some are no longer living, but I will always be in their debt.

First and foremost are the Mukden camp survivors, who shared their recollections, documents, and photos with me: Oliver "Red" Allen; James D. "J. D." Beshears, Arnold Bocksel, Herschel "Frenchie" Bouchey, Robert A. Brown, Art "Lu" Campbell, Herman Castillo, Sam Castrianni, William Wesley Davis, Charles Dragich, Randall Edwards, Leon Elliott, Val Gavito, Ralph Griffith, Philip Haley, Henry Harlan, Erwin Johnson, Vernon La Heist, Paul Lankford, Eddy Laursen, OSS rescuer Hal Leith, David Levy, T. Walter Middleton, Wayne Miller, Leo Padilla, Robert Rosendahl, Bobby Shoobridge, Ken Towery, Joseph Vater, Robert Vogler, Roy Weaver, Robert Wolfersberger, Gene Wooten, and John Zenda.

The help of family members Ferdinand "Fred" Baldassare Jr., Lydia Castillo, Jim DelBonis, Sylvia Elliott, Patricia Favulli, Randy Haley, Mark "Chip" Herbst Jr., Alexander Paliotto, Catherine Meringolo Quoma, Frances Worthington Lipe, Pete Wuttke, and Suzanne and Sheldon Zimbler has been invaluable.

A special thanks is due to the late Melvin Routt, past national commander of the American Defenders of Bataan and Corregidor, who was among the first to supply me with a continuing stream of data about Mukden, where so many of his friends had been confined, and alerted me as early as 1996 to the odd doings at this camp. My thanks also to former POW Wayne Carringer, who put me in touch with several Mukden survivors in his home state, North Carolina. Australian researcher and Web host Peter Winstanley put me in touch with Mukden medic Bobby Shoobridge and sent me the taped recollections of Dr.

Des Brennan and the transcription of William "Dingle" Bell's colorful remembrances, for which I am very thankful.

A special place in heaven must be reserved for Roger Mansell, who out of his own pocket and with countless hours of time, patience, and expertise has created an extraordinary database of Pacific POW camp rosters and archival information, which he has selflessly shared with all of us. Roger's roster of Mukden POWs, their ranks, where they fought prior to capture, and which hellships they traveled on has been priceless to me. Wes Injerd is another wonder resource, especially with current news articles about ex-POWs; he effortlessly clarifies details about the Pacific war.

To me the greatest archive on the planet is the National Archives in Washington, D.C., and its Modern Military Records facility at College Park, Maryland, where I spent many hours, assisted by the incredible depth of knowledge shared with me by senior archivists Richard Boylan, William Cunliffe, Richard Myers, and David van Tassel, along with Mukden record wunderkind Eric vanSlander. I will always be grateful for their expertise in locating just the records I needed, and for the late, legendary John E. Taylor, who put me in touch with everyone else.

It was Richard Myers who suggested my name as a historical advisor to the Nazi War Crimes and Japanese Imperial Records Interagency Working Group (IWG), an honor for which I will always be proud. Historian Edward Drea served on that panel with me, and I am in awe of his depth of knowledge about the entire Pacific war. Gerhard Weinberg, the formidable historian who chaired our Historical Advisory Panel and managed to straddle Europe, America, and Asia with his encyclopedic knowledge, is another source of wonder to me. I appreciate the interest IWG chair Steven Garfinkel has taken in my research and writing. IWG member Eli Rosenbaum, who heads the Office of Special Investigations at the Justice Department, deserves my special thanks for his constant encouragement.

And where would my Pacific war documentation be without the declassification efforts of National Security Agency historian Robert Hanyok? I owe him much for bringing so many valuable files to light in recent years. James Zobel, curator at the MacArthur Memorial, has come to my rescue with lightning speed on many occasions.

Chinese historian and Shenyang native Jing Yang is a sleuth of the highest order. His incredible work in rediscovering and identifying the remains of the Mukden POW camp has been the linchpin of this book. And then he discovered and photographed the small village in Inner Mongolia where the three escaped POWs were recaptured. More recently he has done more than anyone else to solve the mystery of the unaccounted-for Mukden POW, SSgt. William

Lynch, and what may have been his fate in a distant *Kempeitai* prison following his recapture.

Another Shenyang native, Ao Wang, along with his wife Pat, has pushed relentlessly to get local Chinese officials to establish and fund a museum at the Mukden camp site; the couple has formed an organization to serve as liaison between the ex-POWs and museum officials. It is inspiring to see the zeal and determination of Moore's Marauders founder Ken Moore and the group of forensic, archaeological, and geneaology experts he has assembled to locate and retrieve Staff Sergeant Lynch's remains and to return them to his family.

Genealogical supersleuth Marie Daly is a wonder. Her privately funded organization may yet write the final chapter to *Guests of the Emperor*. Mary Kay Wallace, director of the Brooke County Public Library in Wellsburg, West Virginia, has set up a splendid POW museum and resource center in cooperation with the past national commander of the ADBC, Edward Jackfert, and the store of data, photos, and documents he assembled about the Pacific POW experience. I am grateful that her staff has created a Web page for me on their site. And they found just the photos from Joseph Vater's donated collection that I needed for this book. Japanese researchers Shoji Kondo, Fuyuko Nishisato, and Yuka Ibuki provided much valuable data to me.

This work would never have taken its final shape without the skill and guidance of my editor, Adam Kane, the helpful staff at the Naval Institute Press, and their remarkable copy editor, Karin Kaufman. Thank you, all.

Introduction

After the Japanese attacked the American base at Pearl Harbor, Hawaii, early in the morning on Sunday, December 7, 1941 (December 8 in the Pacific Time Zone), the Imperial Japanese Army and Navy swept through Southeast Asia with breathtaking speed, surprising American, British, Australian, and Dutch military units and civilian populations with well-coordinated timing and blunt brutality. Despite being poorly equipped and often poorly led, American soldiers, sailors, and Marines put up a valiant fight, holding off overwhelming Japanese forces for nearly six months. Trapped on the Bataan peninsula on the Philippine island of Luzon, the Americans saw their numbers, their food, and their ammunition dwindle. Finally, on April 9, 1942, the exhausted, sick, and starving men of Bataan surrendered to the Japanese. Barely a month later, on May 6, nearly two thousand soldiers and Marines on the nearby island of Corregidor were also forced to surrender.

Within six months of the attack on Pearl Harbor, Gen. Douglas MacArthur's entire Army of the Pacific, some 78,000 American and Filipino men, had either been killed or captured by Japanese forces. Never in our military history had so many Americans been captured at one time.

Racked with disease and lacking food and water, the prisoners captured on Bataan were forced to march sixty-five miles north to San Fernando and transported from there farther north to Cabanatuan, where they were soon joined by the remnants of Corregidor defenders. By October 1942, nearly five thousand Americans had perished at Cabanatuan; many became convinced they would all die if they had to stay there much longer.

One of the first things the Japanese forced their American captives to do was to fill out a questionnaire stating what unit they had been assigned to and

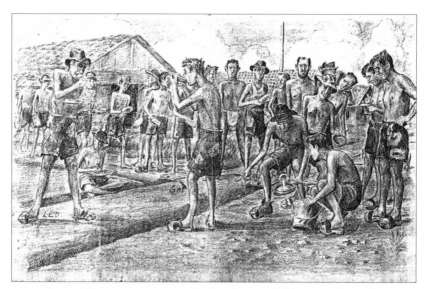

Bataan Death March survivors, Cabanatuan, 1942. *Left foreground:* Mukden POW Leo Padilla. Collection of Agapito Silva.

what their particular duties and skills were. It was from this information that Japanese officers selected men, mostly survivors of Bataan and Corregidor, to fill the Mitsubishi corporation's request for trained aircraft mechanics and skilled machinists to be shipped to Mitsubishi's vast industrial complex in Mukden, Manchuria, including a former Nissan Motors assembly plant, purchased by the Ford Motor Company in the early 1930s. In 1936 Mitsubishi subsidiary Manchu Kosaki Kai Kibasha Ki Kaisha (MKK) purchased the factory from Ford. Ford managers left behind a few white coveralls with the Ford logo on them, which were distributed to the first startled American prisoners who came to the factory in late 1942.

Mitsubishi was the first of several large Japanese corporations clamoring for the use of skilled white prisoners, especially Americans, as laborers in their factories and mines, since most skilled Japanese workers were serving in the military. Ignoring the Geneva Conventions prohibition on the use of prisoners of war for an enemy's war-related production, Mitsubishi wanted approximately 1,500 POWs as soon as possible to work at its planned aircraft parts and tool-and-die factories at Mukden. So anxious was Mitsubishi to receive this white prisoner work force that the company announced it would "temporarily" house the men in old Chinese army huts and would provide new barracks "later."

So in October 1942, when about 1,500 men selected for the trip were informed that they would be leaving their Philippine hellhole, Cabanatuan, most saw their departure as an opportunity for survival. So did their officers, who helped the

Japanese select men for the transfer. Little did they all know that the horrible journey in the hold of the *Tottori Maru,* an old Mitsubishi-owned merchant ship, would cost some their lives, or that the freezing climate of Manchuria would claim the lives of nearly three hundred more sick and weakened American prisoners during that first winter of 1942–43.

Eventually the Mukden POW camp would become the largest fixed camp in the Japanese Empire: 1,485 Americans and more than 500 other Allied prisoners were sent there between November 1942 and August 1945, swelling the camp's population to 2,040 at its peak. How the men of Mukden survived bitter cold, constant brutality, medical experimentation by their Japanese captors, and gnawing starvation while finding ways to constantly sabotage Japan's war effort is a tale of truly heroic endurance.

What makes the Mukden POW camp unique is the mysterious visits by outside medical teams in the winter and spring of 1943 and what they did to some American prisoners during those visits—procedures that would have lifelong consequences for the selected prisoners.

If Saddam Hussein had succeeded in developing biological weapons to use on American troops in Iraq, here's where he would have gotten the blueprints for experimentation: a laboratory in Ping Fan, near Harbin, Manchuria, operated by the infamous General Shiro Ishii and his team during the 1930s and 1940s. Officially titled the Kwantung Army Epidemic Prevention and Water Supply Main Headquarters, the laboratory was known internally as Unit 731 of the Imperial Japanese Army Medical Corps.

Ishii's medical team experimented with biological toxins on human subjects. Nearly all were Chinese; a few were Russian émigrés who had fled to Harbin during the Bolshevik revolution in the 1920s. But General Ishii yearned to test his toxins on more Caucasians, especially Americans, who, he correctly guessed, would eventually try to invade Japan's home islands as Allied military prowess increased in the Pacific. Ishii hoped to disrupt that invasion by finding a way to drop toxin-infested materials, including fleas, on the advancing troop ships. What he needed to do first was develop formula strengths that could be effectively applied to Caucasians, and for this phase of his work he needed to experiment on American subjects. In November 1942 Ishii saw his chance, when 1,200 American prisoners arrived at Mitsubishi's Mukden factory complex, about three hundred miles from Ping Fan.

Japanese researcher and TV producer Shoji Kondo was the first to correctly translate a key 1943 military order from Japan's commanding general in Manchuria, enabling me to become the first to show in English that the medical team ordered to visit the Mukden POW camp in 1943 was, indeed, sent from Ishii's Unit 731 in Ping Fan. Using medical reports from Japanese and POW doctors, postwar trial testimony, and recently declassified documents in the National

Archives, it has been possible to finally connect the dots to prove the source from which medical personnel came to the Mukden POW camp.

Much has been written in recent years about Unit 731. The most comprehensive, well-documented research has been produced by Kondo, not only in his TV documentaries but also in his multivolume 2003 study titled *Unit 731*, published in Harbin. Earlier the book *Factories of Death* by Sheldon Harris became a landmark work on the subject. But whether American prisoners were used in Unit 731 experiments has been a subject of contention and denial for more than sixty years—so much so that on September 19, 2003, the *New York Times* could still note, "If the allegations are true, a Japanese-administered germ warfare program used [American POWs] as guinea pigs." This book removes any doubt.

At a time when prisoner abuse continues to be very much in the news, these pages remind us that starvation, sleep deprivation, brutal beatings, torture, and sexual humiliation were routinely practiced by Japanese captors on American prisoners (who, according to the testimony of other Allied POWs, were singled out for special abuse) at Mukden. Using anecdotes, war crimes investigation affidavits, and personal interviews with survivors, these pages show how a breakdown in leadership and confusing or unknown rules made the lives of POWs at Mukden a living hell—as was true for all POWs in Japanese captivity. In Asia during World War II, there were many Abu Ghraibs and Guantánamos.

But the bitter cold, brutality, and biological experimentation are just some of the elements that set the Mukden POW camp apart from others in the wartime Japanese Empire. It is the only camp I have encountered, in more than five hundred interviews with former POWs from Thailand to Hokkaido, where American prisoners despised their officers so much. It is the only camp from which three POWs escaped, walking and riding the rails for eleven days only to be recaptured—at the edge of the Gobi Desert—because of a language barrier. (Sixty-one years later, villagers in that remote spot told a Chinese historian, "If only we had known they were Americans, we might have helped them. We thought they were spies.") It is the only camp from which a fourth American escaped and was recaptured, taken away, and never accounted for after the war ended. And it is the only camp where a team led by the Office of Strategic Services (OSS) parachuted in to rescue the prisoners—on August 16, 1945, the day after Emperor Hirohito announced on the radio that Japan must surrender. They arrived just before the camp commandant could complete plans to execute the prisoners, and just ahead of the advancing Russian army. Truly, the Mukden camp is a Manchurian mystery.

Technical note: A uniform style is used for military ranks/rates, since the POWs were from different branches of the armed services.

Guests
of the
Emperor

1

The Long Heartbreak Begins

As a stunned White House and Congress, and Americans everywhere, tried to come to grips with the fact that Japanese forces had dared to attack the United States on our own territory, decimating our Pacific Fleet and air power in just one day and killing more than 2,300 officers and men and wounding nearly a thousand more, shock turned to fear—especially on our West Coast. For the first six months of 1942, Americans in Washington State, Oregon, and California huddled around their radios, expecting each newscast to bring word of Japanese ships or planes heading for the United States, especially after April 18, when Brig. Gen. James A. Doolittle led a daring daylight air raid on Tokyo. It was a very vulnerable time. Those who lived through that period can still describe the terrifying feeling of not knowing what might be happening next—to themselves, their communities, or their loved ones trapped as civilians in the Philippines, China, and even Japan—or whether those serving in uniform could survive the lightning speed of coordinated Japanese invasions.

Fears on the home front were well placed: our troops on the ground in the Philippines were poorly equipped, having been issued outdated and even rusty firearms. Their leadership often left much to be desired; it was an open secret that if an Army officer didn't quite measure up or had a drinking problem, more often than not he would be assigned to "easy" duty in the Philippines during the 1930s, where his shortcomings were not likely to be tested very much and well-respected leaders such as Gen. Jonathan Wainwright and Gen. Edward King could be counted on.

As tensions built in 1941, Gen. Douglas MacArthur was recalled to active duty and tasked to organize a command headquarters, recruit and train the Philippine army, and secure decent supplies. He became commanding general of United States Army Forces in the Far East on July 26, 1941. The following month, the region's token air force was put under his command.

It would be the understatement of the century to say that General MacArthur ran out of time, despite the buildup of troops and equipment that slowly got

1

under way. For example, there were seven radar sets in the Philippines, but only two had been set up to operate by December 1941.[1]

When Japanese forces made their main landing at Lingayan Bay in the northern Philippines on December 22, 1941, Guam, with 450 Marine and Navy personnel, had already been captured, and 1,144 civilian construction workers, along with 470 Marines, sailors, and airmen on Wake Island, would become prisoners of the Japanese the following day. The long months and years of heartbreak for American personnel—and their families—had already begun. The anguish of families, civilian and military, became even more acute because initially the Japanese government refused to cooperate with the American or the International Red Cross. Weeks, months, and sometimes years went by before a family could receive confirmation that their loved one was alive and a prisoner of war.

Much has been written about the Battle of the Philippines: how the American and Filipino forces were pushed south until they were trapped on the peninsula of Bataan and how, when Bataan fell on April 9, 1942, those on the island fortress of Corregidor made a final stand, which also ended in surrender on May 6. Equally abundant in the narratives is the finger pointing and blame: how General MacArthur failed to move supplies from Luzon to Bataan, how he kept reassuring his troops that "help is on the way" when he knew this wasn't so, and, in an act many under his command still call a "betrayal" nearly seven decades later, how he abandoned his post on Corregidor March 12 and left Gen. Jonathan Wainwright in command with orders not to surrender.

The fact is that General MacArthur was ordered by President Franklin D. Roosevelt to leave immediately for Australia because by the spring of 1942 it was clear to everyone in Washington that all of the top generals in the Pacific would soon be captives of Japan, and Roosevelt could not allow his supreme commander to be one of them.

But perhaps the most shattering moment for American defenders in the Philippines came on February 23, 1942, when FDR decided to observe the Washington's Birthday holiday weekend by broadcasting one of his legendary "fireside chats." Some troops on Bataan heard that broadcast by shortwave radio, and as they listened to their commander in chief, they knew their fate was sealed. The president began by evoking the image of George Washington: "For eight years, General Washington and his Continental Army were faced continually with formidable odds and recurring defeats. Supplies and equipment were lacking. In a sense, every winter was a Valley Forge. . . . Washington's conduct . . . has provided the model for all Americans ever since—a model of moral stamina."[2] He went on to describe how it would be possible for the United States to help the British in the Middle East and to keep open the North Atlantic supply lines but that the Philippine Islands were now surrounded by Japanese forces and our strategy there would be a delaying action: "The defense put up by General

MacArthur has magnificently exceeded the previous estimates of endurance; and he and his men are gaining eternal glory therefor."

The president next gave the first real statistics the American public received about the toll of the December 7, 1941, attack on Pearl Harbor after explaining the government's news blackout on the press and public by saying that "discretion" is called for in releasing information that might help the enemy. He revealed that 2,230 U.S. military officers and men were killed in the Japanese attack that day and a further 946 wounded, and that just three ships in the Pacific fleet were permanently out of commission. "The Japanese do not know how many [U.S.] planes they destroyed that day," he said, "and I am not going to tell them" (possibly because he also did not want Americans to know how few aircraft we had stationed in Hawaii at that time).

Then the president uttered words the defenders of Bataan who heard them (and not all did) would never forget: "This generation of Americans has come to realize . . . that there is something larger and more important than the life of any individual . . . something for which a man will sacrifice . . . not only his association with those he loves, but his life itself." The men on Bataan who heard that broadcast looked around the room at one another and knew who the sacrifice would be. Cpl. Nick Chintis of the New Mexico 515th Coast Artillery (the core unit defending Bataan) recalled, "I knew who he was talking about, and it was me. I was one of the lambs. Bait. But it didn't bother me. I figured somebody had to do it."[3] His friend, 2nd Lt. Jim Chaney, also knew what FDR was saying: "The Pacific would have to wait. And we knew what the end would be. We couldn't last too long without food and ammunition." Capt. Gerald Greeman remembered, "When the President said we were sending stuff to Russia and the British isles, a lot of men asked: Why not the Philippine Isles?"

Frank Hewlett, the Manila bureau chief for the United Press wire service who covered the siege of Bataan, penned a little ditty that Bataan survivors still chant at their reunions:

We're the battling bastards of Bataan,
No mama, no papa, no Uncle Sam;
No pills, no planes, no artillery pieces.
And nobody gives a damn.
Nobody gives a damn.

Lieutenant Chaney's observation that President Roosevelt believed "the Pacific would have to wait" was borne out later. Easter Sunday 1944 happened to fall on April 9, the day Bataan fell. Knowing that the president customarily broadcast an Easter message and prayers on the radio, the Los Angeles chapter of the Bataan Families Organization wrote Roosevelt asking him to designate April 9 Bataan Day and to remember in his prayers those who had died on Bataan and the thousands who were now suffering as POWs. In a handwritten reply the president wrote, "No . . . Europe first; nothing must distract the American people from Hitler."[4]

For weeks before FDR's fireside chat, the rations on Bataan were being cut back. On January 6, 1942, the food ration was cut in half, to 2,000 calories per day per man. On February 1 food rations dropped to 1,500 calories per day, and on March 1, rations were cut to fewer than 1,000 calories per day.[5] General Wainwright ordered all the horses and mules slaughtered to provide meat for his now-starving men. Leo Padilla, a sergeant in the New Mexico 200th Cavalry, could still say sadly after sixty-one years, "We didn't know we had eaten all our horses until much later."[6]

By the end of March the Bataan defenders were listless and weak; many were suffering from malaria and diseases associated with malnutrition, such as diarrhea and dysentery; and their medical supplies were gone. Within six weeks of the president's fireside broadcast, the forces on Bataan surrendered to the Japanese. General Wainwright could not bring himself to disobey his commander's orders not to surrender. So the task fell to Gen. Edward King to issue the order, hoping to avoid the certain massacre of his exhausted, sick, and starving troops. He had saved enough fuel for a couple of trucks to carry the sick and severely wounded and asked the Japanese commander for permission to use them; it was denied. So the horrible sixty-five-mile Bataan Death March began, with almost no food or water allowed for the entire six days.[7]

No accurate record exists of how many Americans died during the march from Bataan to San Fernando; conditions were too chaotic for anyone to keep written statistics. But within three months five thousand U.S. POWs had perished either on the march or at Camps O'Donnell and Cabanatuan, their final destination.

Meanwhile, on Corregidor, Marines, soldiers, and sailors endured daily Japanese air bombardment and shelling from the newly occupied Japanese positions on Bataan. For twenty-seven days they held out, but this time, under direct threat of annihilation for all his troops, General Wainwright broadcast a message of surrender to all his commanding officers. It took another month for all the troops in the Philippines to proceed to designated POW camps. Approximately 3,500 Army and 2,500 Navy and Marine units were first taken to Bilibid Prison in Manila, then moved to Cabanatuan, arriving there on May 26, 1942. So within six months of Japan's attack on Pearl Harbor, Gen. Douglas MacArthur's entire Army of the Pacific had been either killed or captured.

Before the Pacific war ended, MacArthur's staff recorded 27,465 Americans as military prisoners of the Japanese. But this figure just represents his Army of the Philippines. When the soldiers of the 131st Field Artillery Battalion of Texas and the survivors of the USS *Houston*, captured on Java, are added, along with thousands of civilian workers, businessmen, and merchant mariners also

Map of Manchuria, 1933. Map drawn by Chris Robinson.

treated as POWs by the Japanese, the total swells to 36,260. In addition, 13,996 American civilians were interned by the Japanese, who rounded up every white man, woman, and child in Asia during the first two months of the war.[8]

By June 4 there were approximately 7,000 U.S. POWs at Cabanatuan Camp 1, and another 1,500 Corregidor survivors at Camp 3. It was from this core group of very sick Bataan survivors, and slightly healthier Corregidor men, that POWs were selected to help fulfill Mitsubishi's request for about 1,500 skilled white prisoners to be transported to the company's factory complex at Mukden, Manchuria.

One of the first things their Japanese captors forced POWs to do was to fill out questionnaires stating their previous training and skills. After a couple of months watching their comrades die at an average rate of twenty-five per day, the POWs at Cabanatuan saw selection for work elsewhere as a possible ticket to survival, and so did their officers. American officers helped the Japanese select men with skills as aircraft mechanics or machinists to fill Mitsubishi's search for POWs who could perform such skills at the company's Manchurian work site, producing parts for its Zero fighter planes. It can only be assumed that Mitsubishi executives were not told what these POWs had endured for the past several months or what their physical condition was; apparently their work history was the only focus for selection. By October 1942, when Mitsubishi made its own merchant ship, the *Tottori Maru*, available for the transport, it is estimated that well over 5,500 American POWs had already perished in Japanese captivity. And not all the POW work force selected to fulfill Mitsubishi's quota would survive the voyage to Manchuria.

2

Voyage to a Frozen Hell
and Deadly Camp

The *Tottori Maru* was originally part of the British merchant fleet, built at Glasgow's Russell Shipyard in 1914. It plied the waters of the South China Sea until it was captured by the Japanese at Singapore when the British surrendered in early 1942. The ship was quickly renamed the *Tottori Maru* and became part of Mitsubishi's shipping subsidiary, Nippon Yusen Ko-Kan (Japan Mail and Steamship Company). Mitsubishi offered the services of its own cargo ship to transport nearly two thousand human beings to Japanese company work sites—most destined for its own factory complex at Mukden, Manchuria. Whether transporting cattle, sheep, or humans, shipping companies charged a fee per head, which is why the Japanese crammed so many POWs on board these "hellships," as their unfortunate passengers quickly dubbed them.

The *Tottori Maru*. U.S. Navy Archives.

SSgt. Cecil Dickson of Australia expressed it most succinctly when he described those POW voyages as being made under "unspeakable conditions." Indeed, it is difficult, as one hears or reads descriptions of those voyages, to comprehend the true horrors these prisoners endured on board such ships, which bore no internationally recognized markings (as prescribed by the 1929 Geneva

Conventions) to indicate that they were transporting prisoners of war. It is no wonder so many died at sea, either by drowning after hits by U.S. torpedoes or by the deadly conditions in their fetid cargo holds.

Official Japanese records list 35,279 Allied POWs of all nationalities being transported by sea to various work sites, acknowledging that 10,853 perished en route, including 3,632 Americans—and that was just by drowning.[1] Many more died on board those ships from hunger, thirst, dysentery, dengue fever, malaria, beriberi, or pellagra. No prisoner was in good health when shoved on board a Japanese merchant ship, and all were half-dead when they arrived at their destinations. In his meticulously researched listings, author Gregory F. Michno tallied at least 21,039 Allied POWs of all nationalities as having perished on board Japanese hellships.[2]

At Cabanatuan Japanese camp personnel, with the help of American POW officers, selected about 1,500 American prisoners to help fulfill Mitsubishi's request for white prisoners especially skilled in aircraft mechanics or machinery to work in its manufacturing complex at Mukden. On October 3, 1942, the selected men, along with fourteen of their officers, were loaded on board railroad freight cars and taken to Manila. There they were joined by a few hundred additional American POWs, most of whom were destined for work sites in Japan's home islands. All were survivors of the battles for Bataan, Corregidor, and the Philippines.

On October 6, 1,993 prisoners found themselves at Pier 7 in Manila—the same pier at which they had arrived barely a year earlier. Many noted the irony as they were shoved on board the *Tottori Maru*. Nearly all were pushed down the ladders and crammed into the fore or aft holds. The officers were allowed to remain on deck. Pfc. John Krebs remembered, "We were run aboard like cattle." SSgt. Val Gavito estimated that five hundred POWs were stuffed into the fore hold, with a bit more room to stretch their legs, while the rest, Pvt. Glenn Stewart said, were "packed so tight, we could hardly move." Sgt. Charles Dragich recalled his horror when "a big rat jumped on me, hitting me in the forehead and with its claws." And Sgt. Carleton Edsall said simply, "It was the nastiest boat ride I ever made."[3]

Sgt. Gene Wooten recalled, "We were so crowded that you were forced to sit with your legs and feet drawn up to your stomach. The holds were covered over [while the ship lay at dockside for two days]. With no light or air, conditions soon became miserable. People screaming for air and water. You couldn't move without stepping on someone. There were three five gallon buckets to function as latrines for about 1,200 men. They were always running over. Everyone had dysentery, the worst kind."[4] Sgt. John Zenda also described having to sit with his legs drawn up. When asked if men tried to stand, Zenda gave this chilling reply, "We couldn't stand because we were all so weak from illness that you'd just fall down again."[5]

Pfc. Oliver "Red" Allen made his way to the deck after an attack of malaria hit him while they were still in port:

"The temperature in the hold was oven hot. The men around me were becoming nauseated from the heat and vomiting. Some were glassy-eyed and passing out. . . . I began to have a chill. As soon as the chill passed I made my way up to the deck. I figured if I was where I wasn't supposed to be and got pushed around and maybe shot, I would be no worse off than I was going to be. The ship was preparing to steam out of port when I found an American doctor."
'I'm in terrible shape, Sir. Isn't there anything at all you've got for me to take?'"
"Private, when I came on board this ship I had nothing, but just a few minutes ago a Japanese doctor gave me a gallon jug of liquid quinine. It's a terrible dose, but if you think you can swallow it, I'll give you a bottle full, enough for about 10 days."

Private Allen says that bottle probably saved his life.[6]

Pvt. Ken Towery took the opportunity of a torpedo attack by the U.S. submarine *Grenadier* on October 9, just one day after leaving Manila, to get topside as panicked soldiers on deck called for life jackets from the hold. Towery tossed one up, then grabbed two more and held onto the end of the first one so that the soldier above lifted Towery along with the jacket, enough for him to grab the ladder and climb up.[7] Another POW who clawed his way to the deck was Pfc. Robert Brown, an Army medic. Having found that the aft hold he had been shoved into was loaded with "big old gray back lice," he fought his way topside—another lucky one.[8]

Meanwhile, Lt. Elmer Shabart, a surgeon who was on the deck with other American officers, could see from his position near the ship's fantail that the main shaft of the *Tottori Maru's* propeller was damaged. He surmised "it had been hit by a shell or torpedo." This probably explained why the ship had fallen behind its convoy so soon after leaving the port of Manila.[9] Pfc. Philip Haley noticed something else on the deck of the *Tottori Maru*: the crew had mounted a nonfunctioning World War I cannon on the deck, along with a second cannon made of wood, apparently as decoys.[10]

After the torpedo attack, the ship put into Takao Harbor in Formosa (Taiwan), where the prisoners were off-loaded onto the dock, hosed down with sea water, and given soap to scrub with—a welcome relief. Equally welcome was the fact that the Japanese crew took the opportunity to clean and fumigate the filthy, vermin-infested holds of the ship. Fourteen American prisoners, deemed too sick to travel farther, were taken to the hospital on Formosa, among them Cpl. Joseph Petak's cousin John Urban, who died there a few days later. Each time the *Tottori Maru* came back into port, more POWs were taken to the hospital—thirty-four in all—by the time the ship left for the third time.

While they were on the dock, Pvt. Walter Middleton noticed that "overnight, we received the white printed lettering on our smokestack. I couldn't read it [Japanese], but I was told it said: 'Prisoners of War Aboard.' In my opinion [the Japanese] were afraid because they had Japanese soldiers on board and not because of us. Anyway we got the same advantage of it."[11] Sgt. Wayne Miller also remembered seeing that lettering. This is the only known anecdotal instance of Japanese marking ships carrying POWs in the Pacific. (Apparently U.S. submarine crews couldn't read Japanese either, because the *Tottori Maru* was sunk by the submarine *Hammerhead* in May 1945 off the coast of Thailand.)

As the *Tottori Maru* slowly made its way to Pusan, Korea, in the latter part of October 1942, POWs within earshot of their senior officer, Maj. Stanley Hankins, on the deck recalled that he announced he was now in charge of the prisoners. "He cussed us out," Sgt. Leo Padilla remembered.[12] And SSgt. Art "Lu" Campbell recalled Hankins saying that "he was in charge now, and we had to do what *he* said. But I guess after about his third beating at Mukden . . ." Campbell didn't finish the sentence.[13]

Finally, on November 8, 1942, the *Tottori Maru* docked at Pusan, in the bitter cold, and nearly 1,300 sick, dazed prisoners stumbled ashore, after thirty-two days at sea. Too sick to go farther, 181 were taken to the local hospital; 28 died there. About a month later 153 would finally be sent on to Mukden. At least 23 POWs bound for Mukden had died at sea during the voyage, and another 7 would die before the *Tottori Maru* reached its final destination at Moji, Japan.

Many of the men were barefoot as they stepped onto the Pusan pier, which was covered in about three inches of snow. They were made to strip and given new clothes: warm boots, socks, underwear, shirts, tunics, knit caps, and long, padded overcoats.[14] As they lined up four abreast, Private Middleton heard two Japanese men in business suits (no doubt Mitsubishi executives) saying that the men would be working for their company and that good food, medical attention, and pay would be provided. The businessmen also warned that "those who didn't produce would not be treated as well. We found out later they weren't kidding," Middleton recalled.[15]

The prisoners boarded passenger railroad cars (a pleasant surprise) with drawn shades and given a meal of salmon—their first real food in a long time, which some were too sick to eat during their slow, three-day trip to Mukden. The train stopped at Keijo, Korea, where a car containing about one hundred British and Australian POWs captured on Singapore was coupled on.

On Armistice Day, November 11, 1942 (an irony lost on no one), a very diminished and sick contingent of 1,202 Americans, 1,188 enlisted men and 14 officers, arrived at Mukden to become Mitsubishi's "skilled work force." The sight of a group in such condition must have been disappointing, indeed, to the Japanese camp personnel. By contrast, the Americans noted, the British and Australian prisoners, who had spent the previous several months in far better conditions at the Changi Jail in Singapore, looked incredibly fit—until they all saw their new living quarters.

Mitsubishi was one of the first companies to request the use of white prisoners at their facilities in various locations. In the fall of 1942 the company requested that the chief of staff of the Kwantung Army in Manchuria notify the chief of the Bureau of Military Affairs in Tokyo by telegram 1010 as follows:

> We are ready to intern about 1,500 prisoners of war from the South Sea in empty barracks at Mukden (Peitaying) and intend to make the necessary preparation for a permanent camp this winter and to complete it next spring.
>
> Taking consideration of such conditions, we expect you to transfer the prisoners of war as soon as possible.
>
> P.S. We hope you will indicate to us the intention of the Central Department on the treatment of prisoners.
>
> [Penciled remark:] We will send you the detailed indication when the POWs are temporarily accommodated.[16]

When approximately 1,300 surviving prisoners viewed their new quarters on Armistice Day 1942, what they saw gave new meaning to the word "temporary." An Australian doctor, Capt. Des Brennan, simply called the camp "a real dump."[17] And Corporal Petak wrote that the site was "bleak and desolate."[18] The camp was surrounded by a double barbed-wire fence. The "empty barracks" referred to in the Kwantung Army message were in fact the living quarters of a very old Chinese army training camp, a series of nineteen huts also enclosed by a double barbed-wire fence. Each hut was a long, low, double-walled wood structure sunk about 2 feet below ground and 9 to 10 feet above it. Each barrack was 14 feet wide and 125 feet long, divided in half with an entrance at each end and one in the middle. Raised wooden platforms 6 feet wide extending the length of each side were for sleeping between 70 and 90 men. The floor was brick, and each barrack had two or three wooden plank tables and benches. Sergeant Wooten remembered stepping on those cold bricks: "When we got up in the morning the frost on the bricks looked like it had snowed."[19]

Under a series of regulations issued by the Japanese government from February to April 1942, companies using prisoners of war were responsible for housing, feeding, and providing medical care to their POW workers as well as paying them Japanese soldiers' pay according to rank. Companies were to pay the government thirty yen per month for the use of a field officer, twenty-seven yen per month for a junior officer, twenty-five sen for a warrant officer, fourteen sen for a sergeant, and ten sen for a private.[20] It would be a classic understatement to say that at Mukden these regulations were followed more in the breach than the observance: housing was initially abysmal, but it improved somewhat in mid-1943; medical care was nearly nonexistent, especially as there were

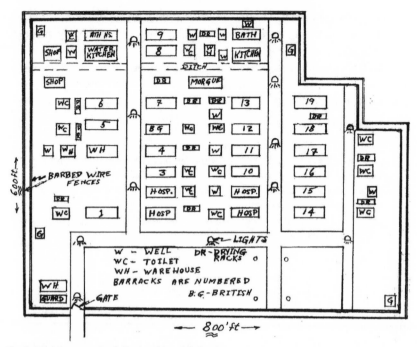

The first Mukden camp site. Collection of Joseph A. Petak.

no medications; food was marginal at best; and officers were paid but the men generally were not.

Petak described the Russian wood stove in the middle of the barracks but said on arrival: "It was very cold. . . . There hadn't been a fire for a very long time." It was the coldest wind he had felt since leaving Alaska. Each man was issued five Army blankets and a mattress cover. When the men started trying to trade blankets for cigarettes, the Japanese guard cautioned: "You will need them here. Very, very, very cold."

"I ain't gonna survive," Petak remembered one man saying.[21] The men were fed watery soup, corn meal, and sourdough buns. Chief American physician Capt. Mark Herbst estimated the men were getting at the most eight hundred calories per day. Petak found himself scavenging the garbage pile outside the Japanese kitchen for scraps of orange peels or bits of vegetables. The men had pellagra, scurvy, beriberi, malaria, and dengue fever. Sergeant Dragich added, "Everybody had colds. We had the same clothes for three years. [He is one of several Mukden survivors who said they did not receive the warm winter clothes issued at Pusan.] A lot of the guys were almost barefoot for years."[22]

When they first arrived the POWs had to stand in the bitter cold and listen to a lecture by the camp commandant, Colonel Matsuyama. Private Towery recalled the commandant's declaration that "the yellow and white man are eternal enemies, and as long as the white man is in Asia, there will be no peace in Asia."[23] Dragich also recollected that the commandant added, "I will not rest well until the last one of you dies."[24] The temperature was around 40 degrees below zero when the prisoners arrived, and the combination of bitter cold, disease, and malnutrition began to take its toll. Between November 11, 1942, and the end of February 1943, 191 Americans died at Mukden. If the count is extended through the end of March, the toll of American dead swelled to at least 235.

However, Australian private William "Dingle" Bell, who arrived with the British and a few American POWs from Singapore, noticed that "not one American officer died in that place. While the other ranks died of malnutrition, the officers got fat. They couldn't eat all that they got; the other ranks couldn't get what they could eat."[25] Sergeant Zenda recalled bitterly, "We found out the officers were taking meat out of the food buckets before sending them to the enlisted barracks."[26] Their suspicions were confirmed when a bucket was delivered one evening with meat scraps floating in the soup. The men quickly devoured the bucketful before a flustered officer burst into the barracks to retrieve the bucket, saying it had been delivered by mistake. "Why?" asked one of the men. "Aren't they the same?" The officer stammered that they sanitized their buckets in a particular way.

Petak recalled one scenario vividly:

> Our food situation was worsening. The maize and the cabbage was cut out and the soupy corn meal was cold when it was brought to the barracks. We banded together and went to the officers who were faring a lot better than the enlisted men. Lieutenant McCarthy [Lt. Dan McCartney] was sent to our barracks to talk to us. The session broke up on a sour note in a bedlam of noise, accusations, recriminations, and name calling. All the men felt and believed that the officers, both American and British, were skimming the best of the food for themselves.
>
> The officers had separate quarters and orderlies to serve them. They had first choice of the food in the kitchen. Some of our men had seen how the food was being separated and rationed. The officers were taking care of themselves first. This caused a great deal of discontent among us.[27]

The high death rate among Americans that first winter was exacerbated by the lack of medical facilities, and in some instances by the seeming indifference of their own POW doctors. In this camp the "hospital" was an empty barracks. Japanese doctor Captain Joichi Kuwashima was in charge; the American doctors were Capt. Mark Herbst and Lt. Elmer Shabart. Australian doctor Capt. Des Brennan was assigned to look after the patients in the Infectious Diseases "hut/ward," as he put it. The hospital was suitable for forty patients, but there were already ninety in it.

The hospital room had a Russian wood stove (*pietska*) in it, but there was a shortage of wood, Brennan said, because the Japanese stole whatever was delivered there. Brennan kept a diary, which he hid under the pillow of the sickest tuberculosis patient. He noted that the outside temperature was 40 degrees below zero and the temperature inside the hospital was 20 degrees below zero. The Americans were in "poor shape, with no clothing worth the name [not all POWs were issued warm clothing in Pusan, as Dragich and others mentioned]. There was no heating, no medicines, no bedpans, and the latrine was outdoors, several yards away through the snow." Dr. Brennan recorded that 115 Americans died in the first thirty days. Many Americans said they were convinced they contracted pneumonia running outdoors back and forth to the latrine. The bath house, which they were allowed to visit once a week, was also a considerable distance from the huts and was so dark the door had to stay open. It was not a popular spot; one POW refused to bathe altogether, telling his fellow POWs that no one ever died of filth. In a taped memoir he made several years later, Brennan exclaimed, "How the hell could we cope? . . . Oh Dear, what a place!"[28]

But Pvt. Leon Elliott credited Brennan with "probably saving my life. It became harder and harder for me to run from the factory to the camp and I became the last one back. A fellow prisoner, Dr. Desmond Brennan from Australia, recognized I had pulmonary tuberculosis and probably saved my life by injecting air into my chest to 'splint' my lung so it could heal."[29]

As if the lack of facilities provided by the Japanese wasn't bad enough, the occasional indifference of American doctors to the POWs' suffering didn't help. Pvt. Eddy Laursen told of falling to the floor, writhing in pain, shortly after their arrival at the camp: "One of my friends went to the officers' quarters and asked Dr. Shabart to help me. The doctor said, 'Can't you see I'm playing cards?' So twelve of my friends went back to demand that the doctor help me. 'Well, bring him to the hospital,' he said. He diagnosed me with kidney stones, but I continued to have severe back pain, having injured my back on Bataan. I was in the hospital until we were liberated."[30] Laursen was one of the first prisoners air-evacuated to Calcutta in September 1945, where fusion surgery was finally performed on his spine.

Private Bell told of a British medic whose attitude didn't help, either. "One man from our hut worked as an orderly in the camp hospital, cheerful type," he recalled. "Every day when he came back to his bunk he had a smile on his face: 'Another four (or five or six) of them [Americans] died today. Hope they all go soon, it'll clean up the camp."[31]

Pfc. Robert Brown has said he was the only member of the American medical staff who was in the POW hospital every day in both the old and new camps because, he said, the American doctors kept falling out of favor with Dr.

Kuwashima, and he would periodically expel them.[32] Like many others Brown praised the work of one Japanese second lieutenant, surgeon Juro Oki.

Sergeant Wooten recalled, "I started retaining fluids and had a hard time breathing. I could take my finger, punch holes in my legs, and the holes would remain there. No medicine was available. Dr. Oki, the Jap camp doctor, purchased medicine for me out of his own pocket. Nephritis—the American doctors told me this. If the Jap camp commander ever found out, the doctor would be in real trouble. He was one good Jap."[33]

With so many American POWs very sick, it is no wonder that a large number—more than three hundred, Private Middleton recalled—could not walk the five miles to Mitsubishi's tool and die factory, the Manchu Kosaki Kai Kibasha Ki Kaisha, or MKK.[34] Such a reduction in the POW work force was very bad for Mitsubishi's war production quotas. By late January 1943, with more than 175 frozen POW bodies stacked in the morgue awaiting burial, the new camp commander, Colonel Genji Matsuda, decided to ask the chief of staff of the Kwantung Army, General Yoshijiro Umezu, to send a team of medical experts to the camp in hopes of improving the prisoners' health—and their ability to work. It was a decision that would have lifelong consequences for some of the men at Mukden.

3

Man in a Cage
The Unit 731 Doctors Come to Mukden

Responding to Colonel Matsuda's urgent request, relayed through the chief of the Medical Bureau of the Kwantung Army, Commanding General Yoshijiro Umezu issued General Operation order C 98 on February 1, 1943:

1. The Chief Supply Officer of the Kwantung Army shall dispatch as soon as possible the following number of persons from the battalion under his command to the Mukden prisoner of war camp and they shall be under the command of the Chief of said camp.

   1 Medical Officer

   2 Medical Petty officers

   10 Medical Orderlies

2. The Chief of the Mukden prisoner of war camp shall strengthen the hygiene service and exert yourself to restore physique of the prisoners of war immediately making use of the above personnel.

3. The Chief of the Kwantung Army HQ shall dispatch as soon as possible about the following number of persons to the Mukden prisoner of war camp and they shall assist and direct the sanitary service of said camp.

   5 officers

   5 Petty Officers

   About 10 men

4. As to the details, in addition to obtaining the direction of the Chief of the Army Medical Services, the commanders concerned shall make arrangement.

   (s) General Umezu

   Commander in Chief

   Kwantung Army

Attached to this order are further instructions from Lieutenant General Kajitsuka, chief of Medical Services for the Kwantung Army:

1. In order to prevent epidemics in the Mukden POW camp, this should be laid upon the importance of examination of the POWs for infection.

Firstly search for intestinal origin, dysentery bacillus, amoebic dysentery of the chronic diarrhea cases which are at present so prevalent. Secondly search for the original germs of malaria and make other necessary examinations.

2. The materials necessary for search for infection will be obtained from the HQ, Sanitation and Water Supply Branch of the Kwantung Army. [This is the formal name for the unit known internally in the Japanese Army Medical Corps as Unit 731.]

3. Any of the above-mentioned research requiring heavy expenditures should be requisitioned for in advance.

Dated February 1, 18th year of Showa [1943].[1]

However, the original English translation of General Umezu's order leaves out a key phrase—where he directed the medical team to come from—thus creating a cloud of confusion, allegation, and denial for the next fifty-five years. For me that cloud was lifted in a 2002 meeting with Japanese researcher and television producer Shoji Kondo. Kondo had a copy of Umezu's order in the original Japanese and pointed to a sentence on page 1 of that order, directing not only the chief supply officer of the Kwantung Army but also the officer in charge of the Kwantung Army's Anti-Infection and Water Supply Main Depot (Unit 731 at Ping Fan) to dispatch the medical team to the Mukden POW camp.[2] So Lieutenant General Kajitsuka specifically ordered Colonel Taro Nagayama, a physician, to head the medical delegation to the camp. Nagayama was chief of Section 4, the Medical Examination and Treatment Section of Unit 731. (It was Nagayama who prepared the medical report of the team's visit to the POW camp, an excerpt of which was also used at the war crimes trials.)

The telltale phrase indicating from where the medical team came is repeated in the 1947 trial testimony of Colonel Tadashi Odajima, former senior official in the Prisoner of War Information Bureau of Japan's War Ministry and a member of the wartime POW Supervision Department. I was given special access to a U.S. prosecutor's personal copy of the International Military Tribunal of the Far East (IMTFE) transcripts in Special Collections at the Starr Law Library, Columbia University School of Law. The transcripts are typewritten on onionskin paper.

In his deposition Colonel Odajima testified that "General Umezu, Commander of the Kwantung Army, taking seriously the POWs' state of health and especially the number of epidemic cases among them, issued special instructions in February 1943 to the Chief Supply Officer of the Kwantung Army and the Officer-in-Charge of the Kwantung Army's Anti-Infection and Water Supply Main Depot [Unit 731] to the effect that the medical service at the Mukden camp be strengthened by allotting or dispatching many medical personnel to this camp, in order to take steps for the immediate restoration of the POWs' physical strength, and to help and direct the medical service of this camp, which I now tender in evidence."[3] It is interesting that Umezu's order was then entered into the record as a defense document to illustrate the deep concern of the Imperial Japanese Army for POWs' health and welfare.

An examination of the original English translation of General Umezu's order makes it abundantly clear how that key phrase was omitted. The translation is handwritten, in pencil, on yellow copy paper. Words are crossed out, written over, and edited in another handwriting. It is a very unusual document, to say the least. Translated documents presented at the IMTFE trials customarily contain an affidavit by the translator, witnessed by a military officer, certifying that this is a true translation of the Japanese-language original. Although a typewritten copy of this translation was subsequently made, marked Defense Document 2003 and Exhibit 3113 when it was entered into the record, no such certification accompanies it. Fortunately for historians, Colonel Odajima's deposition had a better translator; indeed, the transcript records Odajima later correcting some words as his deposition is entered into the record.

The Unit 731 medical team arrived at the Mukden POW camp on February 13, 1943, according to an entry in the diary of Maj. Robert Peaty, the senior British POW officer. Peaty devised an elaborate secret code for his diary and meticulously recorded events, on a near-daily basis, at the camp. His diary, which he transcribed after the war, is the most detailed record of daily life at Mukden. His entry for February 13 reads, "About 10 Japanese medical officers and 20 other ranks arrived to-day to investigate the cause of the large number of deaths."[4] On the following day Peaty recorded, "Vaccination for small-pox." Pfc. Robert Brown, a medic, later recalled that "they came in a truck; they weren't from our camp; they wore white lab coats, surgical masks and white rubber boots, and they stayed about two weeks."[5]

Although the order from General Umezu, the specific instructions from Kwantung chief of medical services Lieutenant General Kajitsuka, and trial testimony by Mukden commandant Colonel Matsuda assert that the purpose of the medical visit by outside doctors was to improve the health of American POWs at Mukden, what the visiting medical team did to Sgt. Herman Castillo proves beyond a doubt that there was an additional purpose for the Unit 731 visits to the camp.[6]

On about the second day of their visit, the Unit 731 medical team singled out Sergeant Castillo and took him to an empty barracks. They put him in a steel wire cage, which he said measured fifty feet in length, three feet six inches in height and twelve inches high at one end, and two feet in height for the remainder of the length. The cage was thirty inches across (see fig. 5, the sketch Castillo drew many years later). He was confined to this cage for nearly two weeks and was not allowed out to bathe, change his clothes, or use a toilet. He crouched at one end to relieve himself or defecate, and he had to stay in soiled pants the entire time of his confinement. Castillo was terrified during the experience—and traumatized for the rest of his life by it. He could not speak about it to his fellow POWs or to his family after he came home from the war.

But in the spring of 1995, Sergeant Castillo was willing to be interviewed by a production team from the Nippon TV network (NTV), led by researcher and TV producer Shoji Kondo and his assistant, Ms. Fuyuko Nishisato. They came to a hotel in Dearborn, Michigan, near his home, and paid for Castillo and his wife to stay overnight so they could interview him for two days. The only two interviews Castillo ever gave about his experience in the cage were to the Japanese TV crew and to me in preparation for writing this book.

At the request of the NTV team, Castillo laboriously drew a sketch of the cage in which he was confined. Nishisato described the great effort with which Castillo made this sketch: "He did so with a great difficulty, because his vision was impaired; he took a long time to do the sketch, with his face so close to the table that it rubbed the surface."[7]

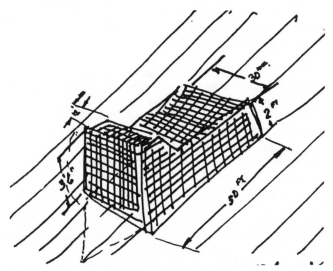

Sgt. Herman Castillo's sketch of his cage at Mukden. Collection of Fuyuko Nishisato.

Castillo told his Japanese interviewers that the Japanese medical personnel sprayed something into his mouth, moved a bird feather in front of his nose, injected powder into his mouth, and inserted a glass rod into his anus. During those two weeks he had fever and chills, vomited, and had dysentery—all without being allowed out of the cage. "At the time I felt I was being used as a human guinea pig," Castillo said. "I knew [the Japanese medical team] came from outside, but I didn't know who they were and where they were from. It was when I learned the nature of Unit 731 [many years later] that the intention they had revealed itself to me."[8]

In a May 2003 interview Castillo told me that a member of the Japanese medical team came to his cage three times during that period "to see if I was still alive" and left without saying anything. At the end of his ordeal, Castillo said the same doctor came and gave him another injection then released him, patted him on the back, and said, "Now you're a carrier for life." When asked if he had inquired, "Carrier of what?" Castillo replied, "I was too upset to ask."[9] He stumbled back to his barracks and did not discuss his ordeal with anyone.

Castillo's wife Lydia told me that Herman had only been married to her for five years when he had to forfeit his driver's license due to poor eyesight, at the age of thirty-five. She drove him to his engineering jobs, first at Temprite then later at Eaton, Yale and Towne, for the next twenty-five years until he retired. He wrote a memoir but forbade his family to read it "until after I'm gone." It was never published. "Herman never wanted to discuss his Mukden experience with anyone," Lydia Castillo said.[10] Sgt. Herman Castillo died in April 2005, after a lifetime of chronic, mysterious illnesses.

While Sergeant Castillo was enduring the first days of his nightmare as a caged animal, his commanding officer, Maj. Stanley Hankins, wrote a "Letter of Thanks to the Chief of the POW Camp, Mukden" on February 17, 1943:

1. On behalf of all the American prisoners of war here in this camp, I wish to express my gratitude for the efforts made by all the personnel who are engaged in health inspections for the purpose of investigating the causes and the present conditions of our bad health, and thereby deciding measures for its improvement and cure.

2. All of us are much impressed by the most painstaking and thorough-going method and attitude taken by these experts. We believe that in spite of the difficulty of their task they will surely achieve satisfactory results.

3. We have received very kind treatment since we came to this camp. It was beyond our expectation to have such concern shown for our welfare [despite the fact that at least 186 Americans had died in the camp so far]. I firmly believe that all of us concerned are so grateful that they will never throughout their lives forget this experience.[11]

It is impossible to know whether Major Hankins wrote that last sentence in irony, but his letter provided the defense with another opportunity at the Tokyo War Crimes Trials to prove their "kindness" toward POWs. Major Hankins' letter was introduced at the trial by an American attorney representing Japanese defendants being questioned regarding the mistreatment of prisoners of war. Apparently neither the American nor British senior POW officer was aware of what was happening to Sergeant Castillo at the time or what happened later to SSgt. Art Campbell and eight other American prisoners, who were called out by their POW numbers in what seemed like a random selection, taken to another empty barrack at the end of the camp, and kept there for nearly two weeks in June.

In an interview with the same Japanese NTV producers at the annual convention of the American Defenders of Bataan and Corregidor in Braintree, Massachusetts, in the spring of 1995 (prior to the television crew's departure for Michigan to interview Castillo), Campbell gave the following narrative, which Nishisato recorded: "In mid-winter, a group of men in white came. I thought they must be Japanese doctors, and medics. First, they gave various tests on [all of] us. They also drew our blood, did examinations of urine and saliva. The next day they brought a basketful of oranges. We all lacked in vitamins and suffered from scabies, inflammation on mouth corners, and stomatitis. [We were told] 'A half of orange, each with vitamin, will solve the problems caused by the shortage of vitamins.' We happily ate these oranges. Those fucking oranges had got germs on them."[12]

Major Peaty's February 18 diary entry notes, "The medical investigation is still in progress. Inspection by a Lieut. Gen. of the Japanese Medical Corps [Kajitsuka]. Many high-ranking officers have inspected us since our arrival. The purpose of their visits seems, as a rule, to be mere curiosity, for we do not observe that anything happens as a result of their inspections except in the case of the fruit [oranges]." And on February 20: "Factory work was suspended while everyone was tested to find carriers and sufferers from dysentery and diarrhea."[13]

Pvt. Walter Middleton was one of at least three hundred Americans who became very ill with dysentery after receiving the shots: "The worst cases—the sickest—were taken to an empty barracks because the Japs had said the ones who couldn't work would not be treated as well. They fed us only once a day."[14] Indeed, at that point very few Americans *could* walk the five miles to the factory. A few days earlier Peaty had noted that "407 men went to the factory, highest number yet."[15]

Cpl. Robert Wolfersberger also recalled how many American POWs got sicker after receiving those inoculations: "I remember that very specifically. About a dozen young Japanese doctors came to our barracks of at least fifty men. They wore masks, and had clipboards. They told us they were medical students from Tokyo.[16] They made us strip—that just made us more miserable in those unheated barracks. They took many body measurements on all of us—hips, skull, etc., using calipers. Then they gave us all shots. We asked what they were, and they told us it was vaccine for flu or something. Some people complained of not feeling good afterwards. None of us felt very good—we were hungry all the time and felt quite miserable anyway, we couldn't keep clean, there were lice—but some felt worse than others. I felt nothing devastating. Dysentery was probably more severe [after the shots]. I just remember that one visit by the Japanese medical team."

Asked if he had discussed this visit with other POWs, Wolfersberger said no. "We were at the mercy of our captors," he explained. "I took one day at a time.

I didn't want to talk about the medical team visit because it just stirred up my memories about it. I just had such bitter hatred for the Japanese; I just wanted to live to get revenge on them. I don't feel that way any more, but I did then."[17]

Sgt. Paul Lankford also recalled the February visit to his barracks of thirty to forty men by a dozen Japanese medical personnel: "We weren't completely well. Two men could only walk fifteen yards at a time with a coal scuttle. We were stripped; a stethoscope was used to listen to our heart. Our eyes and ears were examined. Blood samples were taken by slitting our ear lobes to reduce the pain. We were given shots; they didn't say what for. Very few of the Japanese doctors spoke English. After the shots, many men got sick, and a lot died."[18] SSgt. David Levy remembered at least six Japanese doctors coming for one day to his barracks of forty to fifty men. "They gave us shots and were speaking Japanese. We didn't know what they were saying. One thing they asked was how was my ear wax."[19]

One of the most frightening aspects of this visit by the Unit 731 medical team occurred at night while the men were sleeping. Fifty-six years later Pvt. William Wesley Davis still had vivid memories of those nocturnal intrusions:

> I was asleep on a straw mat on a platform [our beds] in our barracks. At about 4:00 A.M. I was awakened by a tickling sensation. I awoke with a start to see the face of a Japanese unfamiliar to me [i.e., not one of the Mitsubishi company employees or guards he knew by sight], holding a feather under my nose. When I awoke he quickly said, "Excuse me" and moved away, before I could ask what he was doing. Later the men compared notes and we found similar experiences had occurred to others: waking in the middle of the night to find an unfamiliar Japanese face moving among us—sometimes with the feathers, at other times tying a tag with a number on it on a man's toe. In each instance, when the Japanese saw that we had awakened, he would say, "Excuse me" and move on before we could ask for an explanation of what he was doing. We all believed they were trying to take us by surprise and to do things to us while we were asleep.[20]

In a June 1999 letter, Marie Bridges described what her husband, Cpl. Wilson Bridges, had told her prior to his death in 1984. She said he recounted how three men had slept close to one another, sharing blankets and body heat to stay a little warmer. Corporal Bridges slept in the middle. He said that many nights in a row, some Japanese men would come in and give shots to the two men on the outside, and in the morning both would be dead.[21]

It is difficult to ascertain which barracks were targeted for visits by the Unit 731 medical team because after fifty to sixty years, many men cannot recall such details of the "old camp." But the most consistent numbers that turn up are Barracks 5 and 19. For example, Cpl. Robert Vogler remembered that he was in Barrack 19 and that the men on his side of the barrack were taken to an empty barrack by a medical team wearing white smocks, masks, and shiny white boots.

They were given shots with dull needles and the glass rod anal test.[22] The team often visited just one side of a barracks, which were divided by a partition; each side housed between forty and fifty men. This helps explain why some men knew nothing about others being singled out or removed to an empty barrack for days at a time. And men were fearful of calling attention to themselves by discussing such experiences.

On February 24 Major Peaty recorded in his diary, "The medical inspection is completed. The findings are that 'ordinary diarrhea, not usually fatal, plus malnutrition and poor sanitation, and insufficient medicine, have proved a fatal combination of circumstances.'"

Three days earlier, the Unit 731 medical team had overseen the compilation of the monthly medical report for the Mukden camp. As noted earlier, "Mr." (Colonel) Nagayama, who prepared the detailed clinical analysis, was chief of the Medical Examination and Treatment Section of Unit 731. Dated February 21, 1942, the Monthly Medical Report of the Mukden POW Camp begins,

I. Situation of the work: the temporal Prevention Epidemic Squad of the Kuan-Tung [sic; spelling used by IMTFE translator] Water supply and Purification Department organized according to No. 98, C. of the Kuan-Tung Army General Work Order, arrived in Mukden on February 14th, and the practical work was opened on 18th. . . . The pathogens of all prisoners was investigated.

II. Conditions of the patients:
Diarrhea—patients are 247 among 1305, total number of prisoners. . . . Those who were put in isolation-ward as diarrhea patients through the diagnosis of the Surgeon of the POW Camp are 124 . . . other 125 patients [with milder symptoms] who had diarrhea are living together with men of healthy condition. . . . The number of the dead from February 13th to 21st was five.

III. Situation of the pathogens—investigation:
For 124 patients who were in isolated ward [conditions, it] is as follows:

Pathogen	# of positive patients	% examined
Dysentery bacteria	33	26%
Dysentery ameba	15	12%
Trico mucus	11	9%
Xylo mucus	1	

About the clinic situation of so called malnutrition-patients in the Mukden POW Camp Feb. 17th:
Mr. Nagayama, the Chief of the Medical Section [compiled this analysis]
Anglo American officers and men surrendered and taken captive by the formidable onslaught of the Japanese army at Corregidor and Bataan were in a condition of being extremely worn out by desperative fight, lacking in food-materials and suffering from pestilence. For a certain purpose, it was

decided that 1405 prisoners of them be put in the Mukden POW camp.²³ Since December of last year, they were in transportation and during the difficult voyage, being consistently menaced by enemy's submarines the food-supply turned out inevitably very bad; consequently the health-situation of prisoners became much worse, and on the way, at Fushan and other places, 57 persons died. At present, those who are under treatment in the squad are 160 persons, epidemic-patients (mainly A type para-typhus) in the Mukden Military Hospital are 8 persons and those who are healthy and engaged in daily work are no more than 300 persons. Being guided by the head of POW camp and his subordinates, I examined the general clinic situation of patients in the squad with Mr. Tomura, the chief of the squad, and also being guided by Lieutenant [actually Captain] surgeon Kuwashima and sublieutenant surgeon Oki of the squad and in company of Surgeon Major Kobayashi and others who had come for a study and prisoner-surgeons of America and Britain as assistants examined in detail about 20 cases of typical diseases among in-patients.²⁴

There followed a detailed description of the elements of examination of the patients. But this report is as remarkable for what it omits as it is for what it details. Although the condition of the American POWs upon capture is described in some detail, as well as an outline of the conditions during their month-long voyage and the resultant deaths en route to the Mukden camp, no mention is made of the high number of American deaths that had occurred between arrival on November 11, 1942, and the February 1943 medical visit. Nor does the report mention the primitive conditions in this "temporary" camp; the unheated barracks of the old Chinese army huts; the distance to outdoor latrines in temperatures of 40 degrees below zero, which resulted in deaths from pneumonia and exposure; the starvation-level food rations; and the lack of medicines at the POW hospital—all of which were clearly discernible to the visiting medical personnel. And although the report details clinical examination of POWs and hospital patients, no mention is made of the isolation of Herman Castillo in a cage or the night visits to the POW barracks. These details apparently remained recorded in Unit 731's internal documents, which have never been made public. However, the February Monthly Medical Report of the Mukden POW camp remains a revealing window on the Unit 731 visits to Mukden. It has survived nearly intact as a public document because excerpts were used at the Tokyo War Crimes Trials to show efforts on the part of the Imperial Japanese Army to "improve the health" of the American POWs at Mukden. Indeed, the February visit of Unit 731 medical personnel to Mukden had lifelong health consequences for many of the POWs, but improvement was not, as a rule, achieved.

In less than two months the Unit 731 team would pay a return visit to the Mukden camp. Meanwhile the death toll among Americans mounted daily.

Unit 731 Doctors Call Again and Again

On April 19, 1943, Maj. Robert Peaty wrote in his secret camp diary, "Another Japanese medical investigation started today, as apparently the findings of the first did not meet with approval." Peaty only became aware of the return visit by the "outside doctors" three days after they arrived at Mukden POW camp on April 16, according to the camp commander's Monthly Medical Report filed with Tokyo. Of course, the senior British officer at Mukden POW camp had no way of knowing that this second visit was by a Unit 731 medical team, timed to be just eight weeks after the first, primarily to follow up on the progress of their earlier tests on and examinations of American prisoners. According to the camp commander's April 1943 monthly medical report, on this second visit by the Sanitation and Water Supply Squad of the Kwantung Army, the squad of medical personnel "organized its second special inspection corps for our camp."[1] The team stayed for five days.

This time the medical team didn't put any POWs in a cage, as they had done with Sgt. Herman Castillo in February. But they singled out SSgt. Art Campbell, Sgt. Leo Padilla, TSgt. Joseph "Whitey" Sadler, Pfc. Paul Gruber, and five other American POWs, wrote down their POW camp identification numbers, then returned them to the ranks. They would be called out again when the team returned for its final visit to the camp in June.

An excerpt from the April Monthly Medical Report states, under the heading of "Health," "For the prevention of epidemics, the third-term preventive measures were carried out continuing from the previous month. The Sanitation and Water Supply Squad of the Kwantung Army organized its Second Special Inspection Corps for our camp. The corps carried out its examination of feces and serum and skin reaction, starting their work from April 16. The results show an overwhelming number of cases of negative reaction. . . . We therefore closed the third-term preventive measures."[2] The report notes that only in-patients (at the POW hospital) were examined twice. But members of the team did visit the sickest diarrhea sufferers, including Pvt. Walter Middleton, who had been isolated in a separate barrack during the February medical visit. Middleton remembered that during the April visit, "they came to give us vitamin shots. I was weak and lying in my bunk. I could smell the vitamin in the syringe, and the doctor had only one dose left. I did a knuckle trick, which interested him, and when he asked me to do it again, I said 'Give me the shot first.' He did, and then came back to give me more on subsequent days. Two [medical] officers came by and he was with them. He told them about my trick and at first I didn't understand he wanted me to do it again for them. I was sick for a long time. I didn't mention it to anyone until I got to the hospital in North Carolina in 1945. I had amoebic dysentery medicine for ten days."[3]

The medical team apparently brought no supply of medicines with them, much to the dismay of Major Peaty, who noted in his diary on May 23, after the team had left, "While awaiting medicine for diarrhea (which was not forthcoming), men were ordered to exercise by playing baseball. The ball could not be found." This novel therapy was ordered by Captain Kuwashima, the senior camp doctor. His ineffective therapies were described in more detail by 1st Lt. William Thompson, who at the request of Major Hankins wrote an extensive report of camp life after the prisoners were liberated in August 1945. After the war, when he was promoted to the rank of captain, he went up the chain of command for permission to publish his history (which he never did). Thompson wrote:

> At this time, the Japanese doctor, Kuwajima chui (lieutenant) [Kuwashima actually held the rank of captain] was in charge of the camp hospital. For the many men suffering from malaria he prescribed a treatment which was not often effective. A man having a malarial chill and fever would report to the sick call. His temperature and a blood smear would be taken and he would be given a card which he would present every other day to the dispensary in order to receive quinine. The quinine doses were as follows: first three days, fifteen grains per day; next ten days, nine grains per day; and next ten days, three grains per day. That completed the treatment, and it usually happened that within two or three weeks the patient again came down with the chills and fever and the same treatment was repeated. These doses of quinine appear ridiculous when compared with the American treatment which starts out with between thirty and fifty grains per day. Japanese treatment for other diseases was of a similar scale.[4]

At his January 1947 trial in Shanghai, Colonel Matsuda testified about the improvements made at the camp after the medical team visits. He said the food allotment had been increased and prisoners were given a "special allotment" of rice bran and *chon-a-sho-do*, which he explained was a "liquid made from grass to prevent dysentery. It was given in place of tea to the prisoners."[5] Just ten days before the Unit 731 medical team made their April return visit, Major Peaty recorded on April 5 in his diary that 201 prisoners had died in 151 days, nearly all of them Americans. A few weeks after Peaty noted in his diary that no diarrhea medicine was forthcoming, the Unit 731 doctors paid a third and final visit to the Mukden POW camp, beginning June 4, 1943. The following day Peaty wrote, "Anti-dysentery inoculation." Two days later he recorded, "Diarrhea still steadily increasing." And on June 8, "Second dysentery shot."[6] But each injection seemed to prompt a worsening condition in many POWs.

Peaty did not record the exact duration of this visit by "outside doctors," but one of the first things the medical team did was to call out SSgt. Art Campbell, Sgt. Leo Padilla, TSgt. Joseph "Whitey" Sadler, Pfc. Paul Gruber, and the other five POWs who had been called out by number during the medical team's April visit. (Sixty years later, neither Campbell nor Padilla could name the other five POWs, but they believed they were the only two still living.)[7]

In his 1995 interview with the Japanese television crew, Staff Sergeant Campbell recalled, "The nine of us were taken to an empty barrack at the far end of the camp. They gave us muscle shots with a big and long needle. They told us, 'This is horse urine and has various kinds of vitamins in it. So we'll see how it will go by this shot.'" In 2003, Campbell expanded on his memory of this isolation time:

> Two Japanese medical personnel passed us down a line, giving each man half an orange. They didn't let us eat it right away. They made us hold them to make sure each man kept his own. Several days later if we hadn't eaten the first half, they gave us the second half and let us eat them. After eating the oranges, we all got sick—stomach cramps, diarrhea, fever. We got into an argument with the doctors over this.
>
> One Japanese and one American doctor came to visit us in the empty barrack. We wondered why these particular nine of us had been picked [to be isolated like this]. The American doctor was a drunk. [This could have been Capt. Mark Herbst or Lt. Elmer Shabart; both were known to drink heavily in the camp.] The nine of us stayed separate, in that barrack, for several weeks, until we were marched to our new barracks at the new camp [on July 29]. While we were separated like this, they brought us books, written in Norwegian, for us to "read." At least once a week, different teams of Japanese doctors came to see us. One thing we thought was odd: they gave us tooth powder in grey cans and crude toothbrushes with wooden handles. They made us brush our teeth morning and night. We thought this especially odd, since we had no other medical treatment for the past year.[8]

A few additional observations about the Unit 731 medical team visits to the Mukden camp were made by the senior American POW officer, Maj. (now Col.) Stanley Hankins, who was a witness at the trials of Japanese personnel at the Mukden camp beginning in January 1947:

Q: Colonel, do you remember a quarantine squad being sent by the Japanese Army to make an investigation at the Mukden Prison Camp?

A: I do not recall a group by that designation. However, there were three medical investigations conducted by the Japanese during the first few months of 1943.

Q: Do you know who requested these investigations to be made?

A: No.

Q: Do you know what the investigating groups did when they were there?

A: I am familiar with the report made by the first group, the conclusions of which have been read in this court [the February 1943 Monthly Medical Report]. The second group investigated the same subject. I am not familiar with their report. The third group which arrived during the late spring or early summer [beginning June 4] investigated, I believe, the psychological aspects of the prison.[9]

It is abundantly clear from Hankins' testimony that he was unaware of the ordeals of Sergeant Castillo or the isolation of nine of his own men for over a month, June to July 1943.

Slightly more revealing is the January 1947 testimony at that same commission by defendant Colonel Genji Matsuda, the Mukden camp commander, since he had requested the medical visits:

Q: How often did inspecting parties—medical inspection parties—come to the camp?

A: The head of the medical bureau of the Kwantung Army headquarters, inspected the camp once; the Superintendent of the Mukden Army Hospital three times and the quarantine squad [Unit 731] sent by the Kwantung Army headquarters, twice.

Q: When and how often were quarantine squads sent to the Mukden Prisoner of War Camp?

A: The first quarantine squad to come to the camp, was sometime in the latter part of January or early part of February. The quarantine squad stayed at the camp for approximately one week. The second inspection was carried out in the latter part of March or early part of April. The quarantine squad stayed at the camp for approximately five days.

Q: What year was that?

A: 1943.

Q: Who requested that these quarantine squads come to the camp?

A: The quarantine squad was sent to the camp when Captain Kuwashima was sent to Hsinking, the headquarters of the Kwantung Army on official business and when he, Captain Kuwashima, knowing the health conditions of the camp requested repeatedly to the Medical Authorities there to come and inspect the camp.

Q: Who composed this inspection party?
A: This inspection party consisted of the head of the Medical Bureau of the Kwantung Army Headquarters, and members of the Medical Bureau.

Q: Were they inspecting the camp from a health standpoint, or the facilities for the treatment of patients and that sort of thing?
A: They came to inspect the health conditions.

Q: Do you remember a medical inspection team coming to the camp from Tokyo? [Several POWs said the Japanese medical personnel told them they were from Tokyo.]
A: No medical inspection team ever came from Tokyo.

Q: Where was Dr. Taniguchi from?
A: He came from Hsinking, Manchuria.

Q: How did he happen to come to the camp?
A: Captain Taniguchi came with the first quarantine squad.[10]

A major opportunity was probably lost at this point because the prosecutor failed to ask Matsuda where the "quarantine squad" was from. However, the most revealing testimony about medical visits to the Mukden camp came from the Unit 731 staff personnel themselves, when they were interrogated by their Russian captors, who reached Harbin and the Ping Fan facility before U.S. forces were able to secure that location.

On August 8, 1945, three months to the day after Germany surrendered to the Allies in Europe, Premier Josef Stalin fulfilled his pledge made at Yalta to President Franklin Roosevelt and Prime Minister Winston Churchill that he would wait three months after Germany capitulated, then open up an additional front in Asia to distract the Japanese forces. (The date happened to fall between the dropping of atom bombs at Hiroshima on August 6 and Nagasaki on August 9.) The Russian army invaded Manchuria, moving quickly. So it was the Russians who interrogated the Unit 731 personnel, and they did so at a trial in late 1949, convened in the remote city of Khabarovsk rather than Moscow. That site was deliberately chosen to minimize coverage by the world press; permission was denied to several newspapers, including the *New York Times* and Japan's *Asahi Shimbun,* to cover the trials. However, Khabarovsk was also the Russian city closest to Harbin.

The following are excerpts from the questioning of defendant Major Tomio Karasawa, former chief of the (biological) Production Section at Unit 731 in Ping Fan:

Q: Did Detachment 731 study the immunity of Americans to infectious diseases?
A: As far as I can recall, that was at the beginning of 1943 [February 1943]. I was in hospital at the time in Mukden [Mukden Military Hospital] and Minato, one of the researchers of the detachment, came to see me. He told

me about his work, and said that he had come to Mukden to study immunity among American war prisoners.

Minato was sent specially by Detachment 731 to camps where Allied war prisoners were kept in order to study the immunity of Anglo-Saxons to infections diseases.

Q: And for this purpose tests were made of the blood of American war prisoners?

A: That is so.[11]

Major Karasawa elaborated: "A research was conducted in the unit to decide the reaction of an immunizing serum inoculation according to races. To accomplish this purpose, Mr. Minato, a technical expert, examined the blood of American prisoners of war who were near Mukden about the summer of 1943 [the visit to the POW camp beginning June 4]. About this Minato told me that as a result of the study of blood which was started simultaneously with the experimental research of strengthening the power of bacteria, no distinction had been found in serum immunity between races."[12]

So the Unit 731 technicians confirmed to Russian prosecutors that a major purpose of the unit's visits to the Mukden POW camp was to see if Caucasian Americans reacted to bacterial infections in the same way as Asians. (Karasawa was not captured at Ping Fan; he had been transferred in 1944 to the Kwantung Army and was captured in Mukden City on September 1, 1945, by the Soviet army. His connection to Unit 731 was revealed during interrogation by his Russian captors.) General Shiro Ishii, the founder of Unit 731, had already left Harbin on a special train to Korea just prior to the Kwantung Army surrender to the Soviets. He reached Japan and successfully hid from American occupation forces for several months in 1945–46. During the war the Soviet consulate in Harbin had floated a hydrogen balloon carrying a tiny camera that secretly photographed the entire Unit 731 complex at nearby Ping Fan.

The Khabarovsk trials lasted for five days, beginning December 25, 1949, and provoked shock and outrage among the public in the Soviet Union when live experiments upon Chinese and contaminations of whole villages were described. The trials were discredited by the United States and other Allied nations because of earlier "show trials" in the Soviet Union and in order to sow doubt regarding testimony that American POWs were included in Unit 731 experiments. But the fact is that the information provided by Unit 731 personnel to Russian interrogators supports the diary entries of Major Peaty, the testimony of Colonel Matsuda, and recollections of some American POWs at Mukden, who believed they were selected for testing of pathogens by the visiting medical teams. At the conclusion of the Khabarovsk trials, none of the Unit 731 defendants was put to death by the Russians; all were sent back to Japan and quietly released in 1956.[13]

The Colonel's Rules and His "Hospital"

When Colonel Genji Matsuda took command of the Mukden POW camp on December 2, 1942, from his predecessor, Colonel Matsuyama, prisoners soon discovered that things were about to go from bad to worse. Matsuyama had issued a one-page series of general rules, consisting of seven points, on the day the POWs arrived, November 11, 1942, and had ordered that the rules be distributed to officers and barracks leaders. But it soon became clear that Colonel Matsuda meant to impose a multitude of strict regulations, to which he alluded in a series of addresses to the POW officers and "barracks leaders."

On December 8, 1942, Matsuda addressed the POW officers, concluding his remarks by observing, "Your present predicament was, in actuality, brought about by a numbered few politicians and their unreined ambitions. You have fulfilled your duties to your countries. It is for you to tender in a clean sheet, to work in harmonious accord, to obey and to lead a life of neat, orderly discipline under our leadership. . . . You are to understand, though, that any breach of discipline, any disobedience will court only drastic punishment for you in its most prosaic and military sense."[1]

Three days later, on December 11, 1942, Matsuda again addressed the officers and barracks leaders, urging that "those unable to work immediately should put forth every endeavor to gain the assets necessary for getting their berths [assignments] that are waiting for them."[2] And on December 18, 1942, he warned, "While you are at work at the factory, your sincere obedience to its regulations is imperative. . . . On the way to and from the factory: regarding the leader as my representative, you should obey all of his orders and indications."[3]

Later that month Matsuda apparently ordered that his regulations be "translated into English and handed to each leader." I discovered the seventeen pages of handwritten regulations for the Mukden camp at the National Archives, much to the astonishment of camp survivors. I showed the document to at least a dozen Mukden former POWs, all enlisted men, and none had seen it or known of its existence. Yet they frequently were punished and beaten for "not following the rules." The list of rules is divided into eight chapters: chapter 1 is titled "Regulations in General"; chapter 2, "Accommodations and Salutation" (it instructs that every barracks leader "will be responsible to inform one's subordinates the orders and instructions of the Chief Commander of the camp and men in charge"); chapter 3, "Attitude"; chapter 4, "Duties"; chapter 5, "Precaution Against Fire"; chapter 6, "Sanitation"; chapter 7, "Canteen"; and chapter 8, "Various Regulations."[4] It is heartbreaking to read postwar affidavits by the men of Mukden and to wonder how many might have been spared beatings had the rules been posted where they could see and absorb them.

Pfc. Elvin Davis stated to war crimes investigators that "in addition to the horrible living conditions, beatings, slappings and various types of torture became a part of our daily lives. A man would be severely beaten for the least infraction of the rules, and it finally got so bad that the Japanese needed no excuse whatsoever to beat a man."[5] And Maj. Victor Trask said, "Our primary suffering was from the constant imposition of restrictions and punishment for petty violations and from the lack of any decent medical care."[6]

Pfc. Richard Schroeder testified that the Japanese made POWs hit one another in turn if one man didn't bow well enough. "You didn't have to do anything to get these beatings," he said.[7] SSgt. Earl Guyé told investigators that "in December when the weather was very cold we were told to line up outside on the parade grounds. However, there were several of us who did not have shoes and we stayed in the barracks. We were discovered and ordered out onto the parade grounds. We were forced to run the circumference of the parade grounds twenty-seven times. Before this punishment was completed most every man in the group had dropped from exhaustion."[8]

Capt. Theodore Mullikin stated, "At camp we were often deprived of a meal for some minor violation, such as failure to reach our quota of work at the factory. Sometimes prisoners were forced to run around the parade ground naked in the cold weather for some infraction of the rules."[9]

Pvt. Eddy Laursen gave a descriptive statement about the beatings at Mukden:

The beatings consisted of striking the American prisoners of war in the head and about the shoulders with clubs by these [Japanese] officers and by Japanese enlisted men at their direction. The tortures consisted of ordering American prisoners of war to be confined to the guardhouse for days at a time in the cold weather with insufficient clothing and without blankets; the forcing of American prisoners of war to stand naked or nearly naked in the cold air outside the guardhouse when being searched at the close of each day after returning from the MKK factory at Mukden; forcing the American prisoners of war to do push-ups in or outside of the guardhouse till the prisoner was about to collapse and then placing a saber under his abdomen and forcing him to do more push-ups. These incidents occurred so often and to so many prisoners they were regarded as common practice when there were any minor infractions of the camp rules when Captain Ishikawa and Lieutenant Murada were officers of the day. Lt. Murada, who directed these beatings and tortures, was about 35 or 40 years of age; was quite tall for a Japanese, being about 5'8" in height, had a light to medium build, a light complexion, had eyes resembling those of an American in that they were wide open and not slanting, wore reading glasses, spoke good English and reportedly had lived in San Francisco several years and his father is reportedly still a fisherman there in San Francisco. Lt. Murada was a typical American Japanese who knew the likes and dislikes of Americans and because of that fact, made it miserable for the prisoners and was a Japanese who could not be fooled by us.[10]

Maj. Gen. Albert Jones, one of the high-ranking American officers brought to the Mukden camp in the spring of 1945, had this to say about Murada: "I do know he took delight in reducing our already stringent diet for minor infractions and he imposed a constant parade of sentries through our barracks in an effort to catch us lying down in the day time or such similar infractions. He would refuse to have our *benjos* or latrines cleaned, and in short, he did everything that he could possibly devise to make life miserable for us. . . . He saw to it that our guards pushed us around as much as possible . . . and I hope he is punished for his persecution of us all."[11]

Colonel Genji Matsuda with liberated POWs, August 1945. Collection of Joseph A. Petak.

Count 11 of the charges against Colonel Matsuda at his trial in Shanghai on February 28, 1946, was that he "failed to cause American prisoners of war to be advised of the rules and regulations, thereby causing personnel to brutally torture American POWs for alleged violations of rules and regulations."[12]

But Colonel Matsuda's tactics were apparently very effective. Dr. Marcel Junod, appointed in June 1945 as the new representative to Tokyo of the International Committee of the Red Cross (ICRC), made it a point to visit the Mukden camp on his way from Switzerland to Japan. He was forced to travel overland via Poland, Russia, Manchuria, and Korea to reach his new post in the waning days of World War II because the Japanese government would not allow him to fly over enemy territory (the United States) to get to Japan more quickly. He arrived at the Mukden camp on August 5, 1945. The subjugation and fear Junod witnessed among the Mukden POWs was a sight that, by his own admission, haunted him for the rest of his life. (Junod's full account of his visit to the camp will be cited in a later chapter.) His arrival was not prearranged; he just showed up at the Yamato Hotel in Mukden City with his wife, Margherita, and no doubt considerably flummoxed Colonel Matsuda—a fact evident in the way the Mukden commandant handled his unexpected guest.

Colonel Matsuda's report to Tokyo reveals his evasiveness to Junod's questions:

Q. [Dr. Junod, identifying his wife as his secretary, asks:] Would it be alright for my secretary to ask any officer questions [about] laundry or any other small matters about the camp?

A. Your question is not definite nor specific and we have not received any instructions from the central authority about answering such questions. The camp and the prisoners were not prepared especially for the visit of the representatives.

Q. Would it be possible to speak with the prisoners?

A. Last year and the year before it was possible, but this year the central authority has not given any prepared form for the conversations.[13]

In his memoir, *Warrior Without Weapons*, Junod described his insistence, as a medical doctor, on seeing the POW hospital. It was the first time in the three and a half years of the POWs' captivity that a Red Cross representative had been allowed to do so. His description of this brief encounter is scathing:

At the top of the steps stood four men in shirts and shorts at attention. They were the first prisoners of war I had seen in Manchuria. As our procession mounted the steps after [Colonel Matsuda] the men bowed low, their arms kept tightly to their sides, until their heads were almost at a level with their knees.

In a low voice, and making an effort not to show the indignation which was boiling up in me, I said: "That's not the manner in which soldiers of an occidental army salute."

"No, it's the Japanese manner," replied Colonel Matsuda.

We were taken along a corridor with sick-rooms on either side. Standing by the wall near each door were three or four sick prisoners, all of whom bowed low as we approached. Those prisoners who were unable to arise were seated [cross-legged] on their beds, their arms crossed on their chests, and they too bowed low as their bandages, wounds or mutilations would permit. When the last Japanese officer had passed they resumed the upright position, their eyes raised fixedly on the ceiling. Never once did their eyes meet ours. . . . This was indescribably horrible. Matsuda tried to lead us on but I stopped before a group of four prisoners, three British and an American.

"Is there a doctor amongst you?" I asked, trying to keep my voice firm and not betray the emotion I felt. I stood directly in front of a big fellow who towered above me. I could see only his chin and his stretched neck as he looked up at the ceiling. Not a muscle stirred and I repeated my question. There was still no reply and I turned grimly to Matsuda.

"Why doesn't he reply?" I asked. "Isn't he allowed to?"

The Japanese were stupefied at my audacity, but Matsuda was evidently unwilling to risk an unpleasant incident and he indicated one of the men standing against the wall with the others [probably Australian physician Des Brennan]. "This Australian is a doctor," he said.

I went towards my Australian colleague with outstretched hand. I had to overcome a lump in my throat to get out the banal words: "How do you do?"

The man lowered his eyes, but not to me. It was at Matsuda he looked. It was the Colonel's permission he sought. After several seconds which seemed incredibly long his hand slowly rose to mine. I took it and shook it warmly, trying to convey to him all the emotion and sympathy I felt and hoping he would afterwards communicate them to his comrades.[14]

As mentioned earlier the "hospital" in the first camp was an empty barrack with one stove and usually no wood for fuel, the supply having been purloined by the Japanese, according to Australian doctor Capt. Des Brennan, so that the temperature within the hospital hovered around 20 degrees below zero during that first winter of 1942–43. In addition to no heat, Brennan noted, there were no bedpans and no medicines, and because the latrine was outdoors, several yards away through the snow, many American POWs suffering from diarrhea and dysentery contracted pneumonia after they were forced to make repeated trips to the latrine. Brennan wrote bluntly that Japanese officers inspecting the camp "wouldn't dream of coming down to our hospital where germs might leap out upon them. It is very difficult to make a place which really wouldn't be used for a pigsty in Australia, look anything like a hospital."[15]

Brennan wrote of the heartbreak of watching so many men die from lack of medicine. Major Peaty noted that within two weeks of their arrival at Mukden, eight hundred men, nearly all Americans, had reported to the hospital for treatment. Brennan wrote: "Patients dying rapidly . . . clinically these are diphtheria cases. . . . I can only get 10,000 units of serum [from the Mukden Military Hospital, after a twenty-four-hour delay] instead of 24,000. Pellagra is common, and causing deaths as well as pneumonia, both coming on top of dysentery.... Suggestions for improvement of food, health and water supply are heard but never carried out. It is extremely discouraging to have dip[htheria] patients die from lack of [serum], also dysenteries dying from toxemia, pneumonia and pellagra—preventable to a large extent, but no medicine available that is worth anything."[16]

American medical orderly Pfc. Robert Brown provided many details about the POW hospitals in both the "old" and "new" camps at Mukden, as they came to be known, in a series of long interviews over a period of several years. Brown, who died in 2008, was often unsparing in his criticism of surgeons Capt. Mark Herbst and 1st Lt. Elmer Shabart, who were under the control of the chief Japanese doctor, Captain Joichi Kuwashima, for whom Brown reserved his most scathing criticism.

Many POWs provided postwar depositions about Captain Kuwashima's cruelty and brutality, sometimes directly causing the death of a prisoner; their testimony helped persuade prosecutors at his trial in Shanghai that he should be hanged as a war criminal, and ultimately he was.[17] But for more than two years, until November 1944, the prisoners at Mukden had to deal with Kuwashima. And as Brown noted, the American doctors often angered Kuwashima so that he would banish them from the hospital for many weeks at a time. On one occasion Kuwashima banished Herbst and Shabart because they complained to the commandant that he was falsifying hospital records of the weight and length of stay for a prisoner as well as the causes of death when he signed their death certificates. On another occasion, Brown recalled, Kuwashima banished Herbst and Shabart because they reported to the commandant that Kuwashima was stealing medical supplies from Red Cross packages intended for the prisoners and would not let the American doctors have access to those supplies.

A third American doctor, 1st Lt. William Mosiman, was on the *Tottori Maru* but stayed behind at Pusan to help care for the many prisoners considered too sick to continue to Mukden. He arrived at the camp with 125 survivors on December 18, 1942. But Brown maintained that due to the frequent ejections of Captain Herbst and Lieutenant Shabart, he was the only member of the American medical staff who was present every day at the POW hospital during their captivity.[18]

One of the most consistent complaints about Captain Kuwashima's unnecessary cruelty was his insistence, every time he was officer of the day, that the men strip and stand outdoors in below-freezing temperatures while they were searched for contraband after returning from the MKK factory—despite having been searched twice before leaving the factory. On January 4, 1944, Herbst wrote a memorandum of complaint to the Japanese superintendent, stating that a sudden epidemic of influenza was occurring because of the POWs' repeated exposure to cold during strip searches.

Herbst gave a lengthy testimony at Kuwashima's Shanghai trial, describing in detail how Kuwashima withheld medicine, provided inadequate doses of medicine (some from bottles long outdated), and refused to isolate patients with mumps so that a third of the POWs contracted the disease, including Major Peaty. When asked if Colonel Matsuda was aware of Kuwashima's medical behavior, Herbst replied, "Colonel Matsuda, the Japanese commander, was unavailable most of the time and received his information from Lieutenant Miki (assistant to the Adjutant) and Captain Kuwashima. I was under the impression that they only told him what they wanted him to know."[19] By contrast Shabart signed a deposition from his home in Illinois to be used at the trial, stating, "I always managed to obtain the necessary supplies and drugs. . . . I have nothing to offer against the camp administration."[20]

Because Captain Kuwashima often refused to distribute medicines provided by the International Committee of the Red Cross to the POW doctors, Major Hankins got into a prolonged argument on July 10, 1944, with Japanese camp officers, who insisted he sign a receipt for delivery of new medical supplies from the ICRC. Hankins said he could not sign for these articles until the goods were delivered to the prisoners. After much discussion Hankins signed the receipt, stating only that the items had been "delivered to the camp." It would take a sharp-eyed Red Cross official to discern that the items had not been received by the POWs.[21]

The POWs nicknamed Captain Kuwashima "Doctor Go-Back" because he was so unsympathetic when they reported to the hospital for treatment on any given day. He would refuse to admit them for treatment and would tell them to "go back" to their barracks and prepare to go to the factory for work. As a result many sick men were forced daily to go to MKK, including those with obvious symptoms of mumps, leading to an epidemic of the disease in the summer of 1944, cited by Captain Herbst in his testimony at Kuwashima's trial.

Kuwashima's refusal to isolate prisoners with a disease as contagious as mumps is bad enough, but equally egregious is the fact that on March 7, 1944, the entire camp population was tested for worms. According to Peaty's diary, it was determined that 41 percent of the POWs had worms but that the Japanese informed them no medicine was available to treat the condition. A month later, on April 14, the prisoners were tested again, and five hundred men were shown to still have worms, five had amebic dysentery, and ten had trichomona. But, Peaty wrote, "no medicine was forthcoming."

Brown spoke in later years with great pride about stealing the key to the medical supply closet in the first camp and getting a copy made. It gave him access to the supplies that had been withheld from the American doctors, but often there wasn't much on the shelves, partly because many supplies were appropriated by Japanese camp personnel for their own use. Lieutenant Thompson, referring to his first year at Mukden, summarized the hospital situation: "The three [American] doctors worked long hours, assisted by the medical corps men, and sometimes helped, sometimes hindered by the Japanese medical staff, but many cases were beyond help of the limited facilities and deaths sometimes amounted to five in one day."[22]

The hindrances were extremely frustrating because medical supplies were so desperately needed by so many sick prisoners. On January 30, 1943, for example, it was learned that the Vatican had donated 1,500 yen for relief supplies for American prisoners at the Mukden camp. Hankins requested that the funds be used to purchase food and medicine for the POWs, but his request was refused by the Japanese staff, who said they would supply those necessities and that the money should be used instead to purchase sporting equipment.[23] As a result the camp death toll continued to mount.

Hospital conditions improved considerably when the prisoners were moved to the new camp site on July 29, 1943, but Kuwashima's attitude and the frequent impairment of American doctors continued to be an ongoing problem. In his postwar deposition, although Shabart said, "I have nothing to offer against the camp administration," the feeling was not mutual.

On December 23, 1944, for example, Major Peaty noted, "Lt. Shabart was missing at *tenko* [roll call] and was found flat out in the hospital wash-house. I happen to know that one of the Japanese sergeants brought him in two water-bottles full of *sake* [Japanese wine made from rice] that day. The Japanese tried to involve Capt. Herbst in it, but he is too wily. Lt. Murada conducted an 'investigation' and both Shabart and Herbst were knocked about—Shabart had an ear-drum broken." And a week later, on December 30, Peaty recorded that "Lt. Shabart was sentenced to 20 days in detention in quarters for 'missing roll call while under the influence of alcohol,' while Capt. Herbst was relieved from the hospital for 30 days for 'disrespect and disobedience to a Japanese officer during the investigation' (i.e. he would not give away how Shabart got the *sake*)."

Private First Class Brown remembered that Lieutenant Shabart, would suck on gauze pads saturated with alcohol. He maintained that Hankins, Shabart and Herbst would purloin sugar from the kitchen and alcohol from the medical supply closet to concoct their own crude form of distilled spirits. In fact, Brown estimated that Herbst and Shabart were banished by Kuwashima from the POW hospital so often that they were only there about eight months total during their nearly three years in Mukden.[24]

As Thompson noted, "Morale was raised considerably" in the camp when it was announced that Captain Kuwashima was being transferred to another post. On November 18, 1944, Dr. Juro Oki returned to the camp after a year's absence; his presence was welcomed because he had shown kindness to the sick POWs and had often bought medicines for them out of his own pocket. And on

November 25, 1944, all four POW doctors, Captain Herbst, Lieutenant Shabart, Lieutenant Mosiman, and Captain Brennan, were allowed to return to the POW hospital. Barely two weeks later a sortie of B-29 bombers conducted an air raid on the city of Mukden and a stray bomb fell in the POW camp, killing nineteen men and injuring scores of others. Every medical skill was put to the test.

6

The MKK Factory
Daily Toil, Fear, and Sabotage

W hen hundreds of Japanese soldiers poured into Mukden City on the night of September 18, 1931, the fourteen-year occupation of Manchuria by the Kwantung Army began. That night is still commemorated in the city (now Shenyang) each year, beginning with the ringing of a huge gong in the city square at exactly 9:18 P.M. According to Li-Shiu Lee, a Chinese former employee of Mitsubishi's MKK factory who worked alongside American POWs, four million Chinese died during the Japanese occupation and $100 billion in damage was incurred.[1] Mitsubishi was the corporation that soon dominated the city's industrial landscape. In fact, according to Japanese researcher Shoji Kondo, "Mitsubishi ran the show at Mukden."[2]

One large factory just outside the city was built by Nissan Motors in the 1920s as an automobile assembly plant. Ford Motor Company bought the plant from Nissan in the early 1930s to manufacture Ford vehicle parts. In 1936 the plant was purchased from Ford by Manchu Kosaki Kai Kibasha Ki Kaisha (referred to as MKK by both Japanese and Americans). MKK hired civilian engineer Yoshio Kai and brought him from Japan to Mukden because he spoke both Japanese and English fluently. Kai was born in San Francisco and assisted four American engineers who came to Mukden to help set up the plant in 1936. He was put in charge of design at the factory. Being American, he was sympathetic to the POWs, who began work at MKK in late 1942. His presence became a huge blessing to the American prisoners.

"He tried to make their life as comfortable as possible," Kai's son Kenneth (who was born in Mukden) remembered. "He was able to get them extra food and complained to the higher-ups about the brutality he witnessed. He also looked the other way when he saw sabotage. He had to be very cautious or he could have been arrested."[3] Kai is still remembered with gratitude by Mukden survivors; he was their honored guest at their postwar reunions for many years.

Mukden British POW Pfc. Arthur Christie offered a second explanation for Kai's habit of "looking the other way," noting that Japanese are taught from childhood not to comment on something unless they were directly involved.[4] But Yoshio Kai acted out of kindness, because he was supposed to report incidents of sabotage or poor work he might have witnessed.

Mitsubishi had hoped to import a large number of skilled American POW workers, but the corporation was somewhat disappointed at the prisoners who stumbled off the *Tottori Maru* for three reasons. First, as noted earlier, the Americans arrived in such poor condition that very few of them were initially able to walk the five miles from their first "temporary" camp to the MKK factory. Second, according to a postwar affidavit by former MKK president Tokujiro Kubota, only about 60 percent of the Americans sent to Mukden had really useful manufacturing skills.[5] And third, perhaps the largest, often undetected disappointment to Mitsubishi was the extremely high level of sabotage or theft that occurred daily at the plant.

Mitsubishi controlled the operations not only of the main factory complex but also of several smaller factories closer to Mukden City: Teikaton, a tannery; Seian, a textile factory; Manchu Leather; Manchu Cloth; and Nakayama Steel and Lumber. Prisoners were sent to these smaller factories beginning in the spring of 1944 and were housed in subcamps set up near each work site. But initially the POWs who were able to struggle through the snow in that first brutal winter of 1942–43 worked at the MKK factory complex.

Because so many Americans were sick, a fair number of the first group to make the long walk to the factory were British and Australian POWs. Compared to the Americans, the British troops captured at Singapore, having spent their first months of captivity on the grounds of the Changi Jail in Singapore, seemed positively robust to the Americans who first glimpsed them at the Mukden railroad station on Armistice Day.

Australian doctor Capt. Des Brennan noted that because the outside temperature was between 30 and 40 degrees below zero, "even the nose drips formed icicles" as the prisoners walked to and from camp.[6] Major Peaty noted in his diary entry for December 21, 1942, that "68 mechanics and 187 semi-skilled men went to work" at MKK after a list of POW skills had been prepared. A mere 255 ablebodied workers from a camp population of more than 1,300 was surely a disappointment to MKK management.

Lt. William Thompson described the initial work routine:

> On the morning of 21 December, the factory group of about 500 [*sic*] men and three officers [who escorted the men to the factory; officers at Mukden were not required to labor] started work. They lined up at 7:00 A.M. in groups of 100, in columns of four, and were carefully counted. Men on the factory list who were too sick to work had to form up with the others, but in a separate

group. Here they were looked over by the Japanese doctor [Kuwashima] or the officer of the day. He decided on the spot which were too sick but the others were sent to work. Men who claimed to be sick, but appeared well usually received one or more blows on the jaw and were forced to go anyway. The column moved out in five sections with armed guards fore and aft of each and covered the six kilometers to the factory on foot. The noon meal was prepared by prisoners of war in the factory kitchen and served in the large mess hall during the lunch hour. The workers left the factory at about 5:00 P.M., returning to camp at about 6:00 P.M. The name of the factory was the Manchu Kosaku Kikai Kabushiki Kaisha, meaning Manshou Machine Tool Manufacturing Company. It was called MKK by both prisoners of war and the Japanese for convenience. Chief supervisors of the prisoner of war labor were English-speaking, American-educated Japanese civilians [including Yoshio Kai].[7]

Among the first American arrivals at MKK were Cpl. Robert Vogler and Pfc. Herschel Bouchey. Once inside they were startled to be handed white mechanic's coveralls with a Ford logo on the pocket. Bouchey remembered that the name "Ford" was written on the back of the coveralls as well. Both were also surprised to see equipment labeled with familiar American manufacturers' names.[8]

What Lieutenant Thompson did not mention in his description of factory routine was the brutal beatings that were also part of that daily work experience. Many American POWs gave statements to war crimes investigators from the Army's Judge Advocate General's Office, who came to the camp to collect such information beginning in early September 1945, and continued to do so back in the United States as they returned in the early postwar period. What follows is just a sampling of the affidavits given by liberated Mukden survivors; many more such statements are written in the POWs' memoirs.[9]

Pfc. Richard Schroeder, a Marine, said,

> We were to go to work in trucks, but this idea was abolished for some reason I do not know, and we were marched to work. . . . We got two days' rest a month . . . otherwise the work was seven days. The Jap civilians tried to pull a little rough stuff at first, such as giving the prisoners the dirty work and some pushing around. But the Americans struck back at them, for which the penalty was 30 days in the guard house on bread and water. [Eventually] Col. Matsuda ordered that no punishment would be awarded at the factory, all at the camp. I was one of several on lathe work and we sometimes tried not to do the work we were told to do, but this only led to a beating at camp. We were searched when we left the factory and when we entered the camp each day—made to strip down naked regardless of the weather.[10]

Cpl. Robert Wolfersberger stated that "the beatings for minor rule infractions were frequent and harassing; for example, I finagled some cigarettes from a Manchu factory worker and later I was caught goofing off behind a pile of bricks. I was resting and a Jap guard caught me, searched me and found the cigarettes and then the shin-kicking, rifle-butt bashing to my body and a yelling barrage of verbal abuse, in Japanese, plus confiscating my cigarettes!"[11]

Pvt. Charles Shelton told of his entire barracks being called out at 8:30 P.M. one night: "The temperature was below zero. If we wore hats or gloves we had to take them off. So clothed we were made to stand outside at attention for about a half hour. During this time Lieutenant Ando, who I believe was officer of the day, gave a speech stating that he would make us stand out there until he found out who the man was who had drunk some alcohol at the factory that day. We stood there until finally a man volunteered as the culprit. It was reported to me that this man did not even drink alcoholic beverages, but . . . he was put in the guardhouse."[12]

Pfc. Raymond Adams recalled, "In February 1944 I was beaten by 'The Bull' [Lieutenant Miki, notorious for his frequent beatings of POWs]. One of the civilian guards at the MKK factory reported me for tasting some benzine, alcohol and gasoline mixture. Upon our return to the camp I was called in front of the guardhouse by 'The Bull' and he beat me with a saber, and with a wooden club one to two inches in diameter and three to four feet long for a considerable period of time. He broke this club over my hip. As a result of this beating my nose and mouth were bloodied, my face was severely swollen and bruised and my body was black and blue in numerous places."[13]

Cpl. Bruce Callen recalled the sometimes confusing daily orders for work at the factory:

One morning about 7 A.M. there was a formation of all the prisoners of war used in a detail at [MKK]. We were addressed by Captain Ishikawa, and one Japanese enlisted man who was being used as an interpreter. After the interpreter had finished telling us the orders of the captain in very poor English and a confusing manner, we were asked if we understood, and when no one questioned these orders the captain then pointed to Staff Sergeant Barone and asked him to repeat his orders. The sergeant repeated some of the orders but not completely. The captain called Barone to the front of the formation, and as the sergeant arrived at a point within two to three paces of the captain, he saluted, stood at attention, and just then this captain drew his saber and struck the sergeant across the body, sides, shoulder and back. The force of the blows knocked Barone down three or four times, and he was struck five or six times in all; he was then dismissed and sent back to the ranks, which he accomplished under his own power. Then this captain pointed our [Pvt.] Edward Griffith, and asked him to repeat his instructions. He, too, repeated these only in part, and this time the captain rushed over to a point opposite this man, still in ranks, and drew his saber and began to strike him about the body, shoulders and back. The ranks parted as the captain rained blows upon this man and forced him backwards, so he never knocked him down. The captain also struck this man five or six times; then the ranks were reassembled and all of us were marched to our factory employment.[14]

Cpl. Arthur Wells remembered seeing Lieutenant Miki severely beat two American soldiers and one sailor for minor infractions at the factory in June 1943: "These men were beaten with a board two inches by four feet which rendered them unconscious. While the three men were lying on the ground unconscious, he struck them two or three more times. Upon being revived, the sailor required medical attention for a cut above his eye. . . . The reason for the beating was that one soldier was caught smoking in the lavatory at the MKK factory . . . the other soldier was caught with contraband cigarettes, while undergoing showdown inspection. The sailor was caught with a fingernail file, which he had fashioned out of a saw blade."[15]

Some POWs were able to maintain their sanity by noting the absurdity of "incentives" meant to motivate prisoners to fulfill their daily work quotas. Pvt. William "Dingle" Bell, an Australian, described one such attempt:

> There was a new interpreter introduced to the factory. We did not understand this bloke for a long time. He was to be seen hiding around corners spying on the prisoners and watching them working. Everyone knew he was here, so did a little better work until he left to spy on someone else. The secret came out later. He had devised a scheme to improve the output of the factory by incentive colouring of our factory numbers. The best workers were given RED numbers as workers to be trusted. Not as many guards were needed. The moderate workers wore BLUE numbers which said they were just run of the mill workers, and, needed the same amount of guards as everyone was likely to goof off sometime so still needed control. The slackers, or to use American terminology which inspired the colour, "Gold Bricks" had yellow number plates and needed to be watched at all times because they were likely to do the wrong thing at any time of any day.
>
> The minimum time that a yellow number could be worn was one week. Then a further week of "good" work with a blue number allowed you a red number and more freedom to pursue your nefarious schemes. Of course, you only had to get caught and you got an immediate yellow number for your reward. There was about a 60% group Red numbers, 30% Blue and 10% yellow and about 0% improvement in factory output.
>
> The "Bongo Kid" as he was called (Bongo means number), could not understand where he had failed, instead of an improvement it had actually cost money because of all the work involved in the three colour number plates.[16]

Beginning in February 1942 the Japanese government issued a series of regulations for companies using POW labor: the companies were to pay prisoners Japanese soldiers' pay according to rank. This regulation was honored more in the breach than the observance; at many camps senior POW officers were required to sign receipts saying pay had been distributed when it had not. Often the officer was beaten until he signed, and the company's monthly report was dutifully filed with the Prisoner of War Management Bureau in Tokyo noting that pay had been distributed as required and enclosing the coerced receipts to "prove" it.[17]

At the Mukden camp prisoners working at the MKK factory received their first pay on February 4, 1943, according to Lieutenant Thompson's narrative: twenty-five sen per day for a private; thirty sen for those with good attendance; thirty-five sen for specialists' work. Noncommissioned officers supposedly received an additional five sen per day. "Each man was rated (as to skills) by his own statement at the time of capture," Thompson stated.[18]

But MM2c Vernon LaHeist of the Navy gave a more succinct summary of the apparently short-lived pay arrangements at Mukden: "The Japanese decided to start paying us for our work and set rate at twenty sen per day for a ten-hour day and twenty-five sen if you worked overtime. They even paid us in cash one pay day, but when there was nothing to spend our money on, gambling became a problem. As a result the Japanese quit paying but made us sign our name and [said] we would get the money after the war. After a while there was no more signing and we assumed they just stopped paying. In any event we never saw any more of the money."[19] That is, the *enlisted* men never saw any more of the money. The officers continued to be paid, although reportedly never more than fifty sen at a time. However, Thompson related in his narrative that after liberation, on September 5, 1945, American officers apparently discovered fifteen thousand yen that had been locked in a safe in the Japanese commandant's headquarters. "This money was mainly unpaid salaries due factory workers," he wrote. He revealed that a "lottery was held at the evening [movie] show, and [the money] was given away by lottery."[20] This lottery was presumably open to only a few select officers because none of the Mukden survivors I interviewed had ever heard of it.

Far more troubling than the lack of pay was the daily knowledge, among all the POWs, that they were being forced to contribute in some way to Japan's war effort. By contrast the Germans generally followed Article 31 of the Hague Convention (reiterated in the 1929 Geneva Conventions) prohibiting use of prisoners in war-related work for their captors. POWs in German stalags were routinely assigned to road or agricultural work. Not so at Japanese POW work sites, which were located on company property adjacent to the factories, shipyards, mines, and steel mills frantically engaged in meeting the government's war-production quotas.

Mitsubishi's factory complex at Mukden was no exception. Australian doctor Capt. Des Brennan wryly noted in his diary entry for December 11, 1942, "News of factory work—in a machine tool company, above all places. Machine tools are contraband in wartime—and regarded as equivalent to armament. So the Japanese intend to flout the Hague Convention to which they signed on their country's honor to uphold. Complaint about this by British officers [us] were told [in reply] that [the Japanese] may have signed but do not recognize— very convenient but adds to our knowledge of the race."

Former POW GM1c Robert O'Brien said it best at a September 1999 news conference in New York City. Addressing a room full of journalists, the Navy veteran spoke for all POWs when he described the psychological stress of being forced to do war work for the enemy: "You can't imagine what it was like each day, being made to manufacture weapons of war to be used against your own brothers!" (O'Brien had five brothers serving in the military while he was a POW; several were in Pacific combat zones.)[21]

So whether the work involved making precision tools at MKK, processing leather hides for the Japanese military at the Teikaton tannery or making leather gun holsters and belts at Manshu Leather for Japan's soldiers, producing steel helmets at Nakayama Steel or cloth for uniforms at Seian Textile, or manufacturing tents for the Japanese Army at Manchu Cloth, the POWs were aware that they were producing goods for the Japanese military. Whenever they could the prisoners found ways to disrupt the day's production, either at MKK or at the above-mentioned subcamps to which the management began sending POWs in groups of 100 or 150 beginning in the spring of 1944.

Despite the obvious uses of products the men at Mukden were forced to create, Tokujiro Kubota, president of MKK during the war years, gave a deposition in 1947 for the International Military Tribunal for the Far East in Tokyo, stating, "There were no plans to make the company a military factory, and not a single order was received by our company . . . to produce arms or parts thereof. Consequently, our company never used the POWs to engage in work related with the manufacture of arms or with work directly concerned with the operations of war." He further stated that "Colonel Matsuda, Chief of the internment camp in Mukden, inspected our company frequently and instructed all the Japanese and Manchurian employees to treat the prisoners with charity and tolerance."[22] Kubota lied through his teeth.

On October 13, 1944, for example, some POWs at MKK were assigned to work on airplane parts. They were well aware that Mitsubishi produced Japan's best fighter plane, the Zero, and boxes with Mitsubishi's name clearly labeled were provided for the finished parts. "The men objected vehemently, saying that this work was clearly in direct support of Japan's war effort," Thompson recalled. "They were ordered to do the work or face severe punishment. One man continued to object strenuously; he was put in the guard house. He was released and sent back to work when he stated that he would do the work if so ordered by military authorities."[23]

But it was the British officers who made the most direct and formal protest to the new work assignment. Major Peaty records:

A protest was immediately lodged by Captain Horner and with the camp authorities by me, but I was told that the prisoners of war were at the factory to work, and that they would do what work the factory gave them to do, and furthermore that the camp staff would see that they did do the work. Once again, they reiterated that Japan had never ratified the [1929] Geneva Convention, and was not in any way bound by it. I asked if they had Law Courts in Japan for people who broke the law, and they said yes, they had very good Law Courts. So then I asked if in their Law Courts they accepted as an excuse for doing wrong, that the law-breaker had never signified his agreement with the laws. They said no, that would be ridiculous. So then I said that International Law is the law which governs the conduct of nations, and that after the war, Japan's conduct would be judged by that standard, and that they too would find it was no excuse to say that they had not signified their agreement. Then the fat was properly in the fire! I was threatened with all sorts of penalties for "insolence to an Imperial Japanese Army officer" and so on, but I walked out of the office and left them raging. I think I got under their skin that time.[24]

Indeed, the fat was in the fire, and acts of sabotage at all the Mukden work sites swung into high gear.

Sabotage was carried out by Allied POWs in every location where they were forced to work for Japan's war effort. From stuffing termite nests into the wooden structures holding up bridges over the Kwai River in Thailand, to shearing rivets off steel plates at Kawasaki's shipyard in Kobe, Japan, to punching holes in oil drums being loaded onto cargo ships at Mitsui's Yokohama stevedoring docks, American prisoners found daily ways to disrupt Japan's efforts. But sabotage reached a high art form at Mukden. There are more stories of creative mischief told by Mukden survivors than from any other location in the Japanese Empire.

Always the stories are told with a smile—and with great pride at the memory of being part of America's war effort even while a prisoner of that enemy. At Mukden there were opportunities at a variety of places: the MKK factory, the steel mill, the lumber yard, the leather factory, and the textile and cloth factories. Indeed, new chances seemed to present themselves each day.

On March 6, 1943, the Japanese camp personnel took several American and British officers to a site near the MKK factory to witness the ceremony of breaking ground for new barracks to house the prisoners. Peaty noted in his diary, "As this was the first time most of us [officers] had been outside the camp, the trip in itself was an event of great interest." The Japanese proudly announced they planned to spend about five million yen to provide more comfortable living quarters for the prisoners.

At around the same time, Japanese officers announced that a new factory would be built alongside the present one and that the prisoners would participate in its construction. Little did the camp staff know how costly this decision would be. For example, when the guards were at lunch, the prisoners would continue pouring the cement floor in the huge new factory building—but not until they had thrown in every shovel, pick, and tool they could find nearby, in addition to every vital machine part on which they could lay their hands. "None of the lathes were usable because we buried all the gears," Sgt. Leo Padilla remembered proudly.[25]

Cpl. Joseph Petak initiated this most effective effort:

> The shell of the building had been completed and the interior was empty. Our task was to lay out the machine shop for the lathes, drill presses, milling machines, grinders and planers. . . . Most of the machines had been shipped in from the Philippines, Singapore and China. The machines had been manufactured in the United States, Germany and England. It was the booty that the Japs had taken after they had captured other countries during the war. . . . The factory floor was crammed full of [equipment]. . . . "He's [the Japanese foreman] working our asses off," complained S1c Victorian Savoie to Corporal Petak. "He wants all of the concrete poured by six tonight or we don't go home."
>
> "I'll get the Jap to check the factory layout with me at the far end of the building. You get the [POW] crane operator to dump the turret lathe into the pit. Looks like there is enough concrete to cover it," Corporal Petak instructed. "Savoie looked at me as if I had proposed a plan to blow up the Imperial Palace." "You give us five minutes and it's done."[26]

Thus was born a daily pattern of sabotage in which the POWs gleefully participated until the entire, now heavily reinforced, huge concrete floor of the factory was completed.

"Some of the machinery said 'Made in Dayton, Ohio,'" Pvt. Wesley Davis remembered. "It was stressful making parts for field artillery weapons, knowing

The MKK factory, Mukden, 2003. Author photo.

[Left] Former POWs Robert Rosendahl and Oliver Allen reminiscing at Mukden, 2003. Author photo.

[Right] Former POW Oliver Allen's feet, standing over buried tools at Mukden, 2003.

they would be used on our people. We sabotaged as much as we could. . . . We ruined quite a few weapon parts."[27]

"We'd put metal filings in with the grease that was used to lubricate the parts," Bouchey recalled.[28] "I just remember what we did wrong. The eight balls [those under some suspicion] went to the textile mill," Padilla cheerfully said. "They moved me to the textile factory, but I showed the men how to pull the loom levers all at once and bend the framework of the machines," Davis recalled with pride in 1999.

At the cloth factory, Cpl. James D. "J. D." Beshears said with a twinkle in his eye, "I didn't make my quota for a week. I loosened a screw to the loom and the loom caught fire. While the fire brigade was being summoned, I kicked a little more lint under the loom to keep the fire going."[29] Private Bouchey was moved to the tannery, producing soles for Japanese combat boots. "Sometimes we'd write graffiti on the leather," he chuckled.

Occasionally, the sabotage was a joint Japanese-American-Australian effort. Private Bell recalled that a "railway truck full of food wrongly found itself in the factory siding. . . . Even the guards took turns to steal food from the truck. . . . The food consisted of pork and all the derivatives, namely, ham, chitlings, salami, trotters, and bacon. The only thing missing was the pig's squeal. Just about every-one got his belly filled as a result of this slight error in delivery. In a little over two days about ten tons of food just disappeared and there was no official knowledge of a truck load of food."[30]

Pfc. Philip Haley observed, "The Chinese and Japanese were just as hungry as we were. The Chinese would steal and the Japs would steal, and we stole both of them blind and they didn't say anything."[31] Haley was one of the lucky ones who worked in the main mess hall, where he was part of an elaborate scheme to purloin and conceal extra food. Haley disassembled compass parts to pick locks in the camp and factory. His son Randall wrote an account as his father described it to him:

> Stolen sacks of extra flour and cornmeal were stored in a niche hewn out of the ceiling behind the oven's smoke stack that could be easily accessed by a trap door. In 30 seconds, nearly anything could be easily concealed and hidden from view (even large items). The trap door had a lead weight attached to it, so it would sound solid when inspected. It was also equipped with a pulley so it could be lifted up and lowered with ease of effort. Because of this centralized hiding place, the prisoners all regularly received cornbread with their lunch twice a week, instead of the customary once. This was of course a big thing to the hungry POWs. The Japanese never noticed the ration supplement, nor did they ever discover the secret door. Hiding from the Japanese was not easy (as may be implied by these passages). They were not necessarily incompetent or totally apathetic, but rather victimized by brilliant American and Allied ingenuity.[32]

By May 1944 the Japanese had had enough of the most consistent troublemakers. They lined up 150 of the worst offenders, all Americans, and marched them out of the camp. This caused a good deal of consternation among their fellow POWs, some of whom feared that the selectees were being marched away to be shot. It wasn't until the war ended that Mukden survivors learned to their relief that the 150 men had been sent to Mitsui's lead mine at Kamioka, Japan, deliberately chosen because the senior POWs there were British, known to keep stricter discipline among their own ranks and to cooperate with the Japanese more than the Americans were willing to do.[33]

Still, prisoners at the MKK factory, knowing that they were making aircraft parts to be placed in boxes for shipment to Mitsubishi's Zero assembly plant, adopted a motto: "No part will leave this factory in working order." Some said they took satisfaction in picturing a Japanese pilot attacking an American plane, opening fire, and finding his machine guns had jammed. Score one for the Mukden POW workers.

7

Major Stanley Hankins
A Major Military Embarrassment

The POW camp at Mukden was different from other POW camps in several ways. It was the largest fixed camp in the Japanese Empire, the death rate among Americans was extremely high, there were both escapes and executions, Red Cross representatives were allowed to visit on several occasions, the contents of Red Cross boxes were actually distributed to prisoners with increasing frequency as the war drew to a close, medical teams from Japan's bio-warfare Unit 731 visited the camp three times, propaganda film crews came to Mukden to portray it as a "model camp," the food supply gradually improved and was more varied than at other POW camps, and a dramatic rescue by an Office of Strategic Services (OSS) team occurred at war's end.

But one feature in particular is unique to Mukden: the disdain American enlisted personnel felt toward their officers, especially toward their senior officer, Maj. Stanley Hankins. For more than three decades I have interviewed former POWs who were confined in Japanese camps from Thailand to Taiwan, from Changi in Singapore to Woosung in China, and from the jungles of Borneo to the mountains of Japan's home islands—and in nearly all of these locations, prisoners respected and often admired their officers, who argued with Japanese captors about the camps' brutality, lack of medicine, and unsafe working conditions. In other words officers went to bat for their men; they stood up to Japanese commanders and frequently took brutal punishment for their boldness. But among survivors of Mukden, it has been hard to find an enlisted man who has anything good to say about Major Hankins—or about most of the fourteen officers who served with him.

Stanley H. Hankins was from Kentucky. Like many young men in the Depression years, he enlisted in the Army, advancing to the rank of corporal before being assigned to the Philippines. But Corporal Hankins had also enlisted in the Army Reserves, and by attending regular training sessions, he rose to the rank of major in the Reserves. When his unit was called to active duty on December 8, 1941, following the Japanese attack on Pearl Harbor, Corporal Hankins became Major Hankins.

The Army's WO1 Arnold Bocksel called Hankins "one of the finest officers I ever met." But in the next breath, Bocksel acknowledged that Hankins, a college graduate, was an alcoholic: "He was brilliant—*brilliant*— if you could keep him away from the bottle."[1] Bocksel's admiration for his senior officer was not shared by many of the enlisted men who were selected at Cabanatuan to travel to Manchuria with Major Hankins. Bocksel confirmed that from the papers the prisoners filled out for the Japanese after capture, POWs with technical abilities were given priority to fill the ranks of prisoners at Mukden. "All the officers [who were selected] had technical skills of some sort. We were selected on one day's notice," he said.

On board the *Tottori Maru*, as mentioned earlier, both SSgt. Art Campbell and Sgt. Leo Padilla recalled how Major Hankins tried to assert his authority, reminding them that *he* was in charge now. As Campbell put it, "We would have to do what *he* said. But I guess after the third beating [at Mukden]. . . ." Staff Sergeant. Campbell didn't finish the sentence.[2] But Pfc. Henry Harlan remembered a specific incident from their early days at Mukden: "We all, a group of us, had done something wrong—I don't remember what. The Japanese assigned each of us a number and told us to wear it at all times. Major Hankins came into our quarters, and I wasn't wearing my number at the time. The others were. Hankins called my number, and I said I knew the person, but he wasn't here. Hankins then berated the others but not me. He began to cry and said, 'I've taken my last beating for you boys.'"[3]

"After that," Campbell said, "we began calling him 'the gopher' because we never saw him." Asked to summarize his view of Hankins, Campbell's face hardened as he replied, "I thought he should never have been allowed to wear the uniform of the United States Army again."

Pfc. Herschel Bouchey said simply, "Hankins was nothing. I told him he was a disgrace to humanity."[4] When asked about Hankins, Corporal "J. D." Beshears said, "I didn't have anything to do with him. I don't remember ever seeing him."[5] Harlan added bitterly, "We called him 'Hogjaw' because he gained about sixty pounds. The officers had plenty to eat and we were starving. The Japanese were paying the officers, but not us, so the officers could buy things."[6] Sgt. John Zenda laughed as he remembered Hankins in the camp: "When the weather warmed up a little, we began to see Hankins occasionally. When we walked by him, we'd say 'oink-oink' because his cheeks were so puffy and pink like a pig's."[7]

Pvt. Eddy Laursen summed up the feelings of many survivors of Mukden when he said, "I was disappointed in our officers. They didn't do all they could for us."[8] Pfc. Robert Brown, a medic, was even more blunt: "The officers never

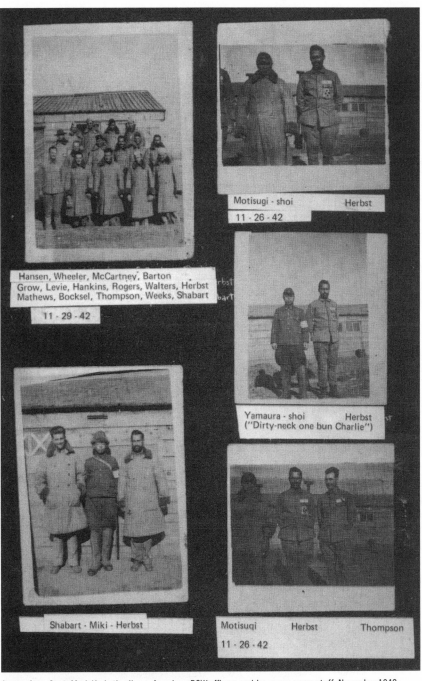

Motisugi - shoi   Herbst
11 - 26 - 42

Hansen, Wheeler, McCartney, Barton
Grow, Levie, Hankins, Rogers, Walters, Herbst
Mathews, Bocksel, Thompson, Weeks, Shabart

11 - 29 - 42

Yamaura - shoi   Herbst
("Dirty-neck one bun Charlie")

Shabart · Miki · Herbst

Motisuqi   Herbst   Thompson

11 - 26 · 42

A page from Capt. Mark Herbst's album: American POW officers and Japanese camp staff, November 1942. Collection of Joseph A. Vater.

did anything for us. But the Japanese assigned some of them to supervise us. [Warrant Officer] Bocksel was put in charge of the kitchen. He hid a side of pork in the rafters and the Japanese found it. They cut our rations in half. We got so mad we told the Japanese to remove the officers from contact with us or we'd kill them. The Japanese complied."[9]

Major Peaty confirmed this in his diary entry for December 3, 1943: "Food has become very bad since Bocksel (an American Chief Warrant Officer) was relieved from his post as messing officer by the Japanese, on November 30. Rations seem to have been almost halved." By contrast MM John Ward of the Navy stated that "W. O. Bocksel did an excellent job. . . . I never did see a man that could pull the wool over the Japs, and wheedle food and other things out of them and with as much success as he could."[10]

Sergeant Padilla said of Major Hankins, "No one liked Hankins. We called him 'Handlebar Hankins' because he waxed his mustache. He had everything he wanted. I never faced the guy."[11] Brown offered an explanation for Hankins' overall behavior and the disdain with which all the men interviewed referred to him as "Hankins" rather than "Major Hankins": "Hankins would steal alcohol from the POW hospital supplies, and sugar from the kitchen, so he could concoct his own distilled spirits. He was a *very* heavy drinker." Which may be one reason Hankins stayed out of sight so much.

RM1c Randall Edwards, USN, offered one of the few ambivalent opinions about Hankins when he remarked, "I don't know of anything he *did* that would have offended anybody."[12] But that remark highlighted what may be the chief complaint about Hankins: lack of leadership. It wasn't so much what he *did* as what he *didn't* do. For example, his timidity was revealed in his testimony as a witness during the postwar trial in Shanghai of Colonel Matsuda: "I was forbidden to speak officially to Col. Matsuda and only spoke of small things when I occasionally saw him. This was on orders from Corporal Noda. I assumed the orders came from [Lieutenant] Miki [superintendent of the camp]."[13]

Major Hankins' letter thanking Colonel Matsuda for asking medical personnel to visit the camp provided a document for Japanese defendants at the Tokyo War Crimes Trials as evidence of their "caring" treatment of POWs. His statements sometimes also provided propaganda opportunities for his captors to exploit. On July 20, 1943, Japan's English-language Domei wire service sent out a story for worldwide distribution:

Heartfelt thanks and appreciation by American prisoners of war toward the generous and kind attitude of the Imperial Japanese Army was expressed by Major Hanking [*sic*], on behalf of his comrades, on the occasion of a solemn ceremony for the dedication of a very excellent cemetery.

The ceremony was conducted at the Mukden war prisoners camp on June 13 and was attended by many Japanese authorities and those who are being cared for at the camp.

Major Hankings who is acting as the leader of the American headquarters in the camp, delivered an impressive dedication address as well as writing a letter of appreciation to the chief commander of the Mukden war prisoners camp. In his letter Major Hankings wrote: "On behalf [of] the American prisoners of war I wish to express appreciation for the privileges and materials which have made possible the very excellent cemetery dedicated on June 13.

"We consider this cemetery and other evidence of the Chief Commander's interest in our welfare, not only as the natural results of just and comprehensive administration but as a highly commendable act. Signed, Major Hankings."[14]

But in his "Narrative History," written after the war, Lt. William Thompson noted that Hankins had a wider purpose for making his statement:

On the 13th, a dedication ceremony was attended by 951 prisoners and many of the Japanese, including Colonel Matsuda, Commandant; Lieutenant Miki, Superintendent Officer, and Lieutenant Murata, Censor Officer. Prayers were offered, hymns were sung, and at the close Major Hankins made a speech to the assembled men. The Japanese thought this speech good propaganda material as the Major had thanked them for constructing 218 individual crosses for the dead. The speech was printed in the Nippon Times, but that copy was not distributed to the Mukden Camp. [It was later learned that the speech was read in widespread prison camps in the Philippines, Japan, and China.] As the speech inferred more than it said, these other prisoners were able to read the truth between the lines, that many men were unnecessarily dying of disease at Mukden. It was the Major's hope and intention that this information get into Allied hands.[15]

Despite his intentions Major Hankins drew growing resentment from the men in the camp. The Americans were greatly relieved when a group of high-ranking officers arrived at Mukden from Formosa in the spring of 1945. Among them was Maj. Gen. George Parker, and he became the senior American officer in the camp. The American enlisted men sought out General Parker to lodge formal complaints about Hankins' behavior. So numerous were the complaints that Parker felt obliged to return Hankins to the United States "under order of court," which meant that the Judge Advocate General's Office would investigate and evaluate the complaints and decide whether to proceed with a court-martial.

In his postwar affidavit Cpl. Leo Rogers expressed what many felt:

Major Hankins, U.S. Army, definitely was responsible for diverting sugar in the galley to make an alcoholic beverage. He and about half the American officers were drunk on a number of occasions. On one occasion an American officer turned the names of certain men over to the Japs for making too much noise in the barracks early in the evening. The men were subsequently beaten by the Japs. The previous night a number of the officers who slept over these enlisted

men had been howling drunk till well after midnight. Major Hankins permitted the mess officer, Warrant Officer Bocksel, U.S. Army, to serve the officers
hot cakes and maple syrup, sweet rolls, beans and ham, food in sharp contrast
to that of the enlisted men.

A Corporal Wantland, who was on the *Tottori Maru* but not sent to Mukden,
stated, "During the trip from Manila to Formosa on the *Tottori Maru* in October
1942, Major Hankins sold contaminated food to the American prisoners. The
seepage from the urinal contaminated the sugar which the major was selling
but a prisoner couldn't buy any fruit unless he bought some sugar."[16] And WO
Harold M. Farrell, a Marine, stated that "a Major Hankins, U.S. Army, was camp
commander at Mukden. He made an alcoholic beverage from sugar diverted
from the other prisoners' diet, and was drunk on a number of occasions."[17]

In his affidavit Sgt. Thomas Proulx was asked if Hankins had protested to
Colonel Matsuda about the POWs doing war work and replied, "Not by Maj.
Hankins. However, toward the end [of the war] a large group of American
Colonels and Generals came into the camp and these men protested very
vehemently."[18]

Even Major Peaty may have shared to some degree the disdain the American
POWs felt for Major Hankins. In describing a memorial service at the POW cemetery on July 22, 1943, organized by the Japanese staff (primarily for the benefit
of a visiting Japanese propaganda camera crew), Peaty wrote, "I did not follow
Major Hankins' example in bowing, Japanese fashion. . . . I tried to remember
how His Majesty the King acts when he places a wreath on the Cenotaph, and
could not stomach the Japanese bowing. Many American 'enlisted men' came
and spoke to me about it, so I felt I had upheld our dignity a little."

When Lt. Col. J. F. Donovan prepared his report as Recovery Team No. 1
leader for the Mukden camp, General Parker had passed on so many complaints
to him about Hankins that Donovan had to include the information in the
"Special War Problems Division" enclosure in his final report. Also, his Recovery
Team No. 1 listed most POWs' health as "good," but Hankins' health was listed
as "fair."

When Major Hankins returned to the United States, he spent several months
at the Ashford General Hospital in White Sulphur Springs, West Virginia. While
there he received a letter dated March 4, 1946, from Capt. Willard Smith of the
Provost Marshal General's Office, inquiring where the records for the Mukden
camp were located. Hankins replied that Donovan had taken possession of individual service records and those of deceased POWs, that Captain Herbst had the
medical records, and that his own "personal diary" and other important papers
were at his home in Hampton, Virginia. However, no one seems to have ever
seen Hankins make any notes or write in a diary, and even his fellow officers
did not recall his ever mentioning a diary. When Colonel Donovan asked that a

narrative of the camp experience be prepared, Major Hankins immediately suggested that Lieutenant Thompson take on that task.

In his reply of March 11, 1946, to Captain Smith, Hankins says that he had been ordered to report to Fort Knox, Kentucky, on March 15 and from there he was to go to Fort Meade, Maryland, until March 25. It is possible that at one of these locations Hankins was questioned and the complaints about him evaluated by the Judge Advocate General's Office, but a June 2009 search of records at the National Archives indicates that no further disciplinary action was taken against Hankins. The Reference Section, Modern Military Records, in College Park, Maryland, indicates that the Far East Name Card index to the War Crimes Investigative files of the Judge Advocate General's Office contains twenty-five records naming Hankins as a witness to acts of brutality on POWs by Japanese camp personnel at Mukden and just one record of an accusation against Hankins: the incident of selling contaminated sugar to POWs on board the *Tottori Maru*.

Richard Boylan, an expert on war crimes at the National Archives, noted that for the judge advocate general, the priority would have been to build as strong a case as possible against each Japanese combatant or official accused of war crimes; thus Hankins was more valuable to the judge advocate general as a witness for the prosecution, and complaints about him by POWs would have been of secondary importance. And, indeed, Hankins was brought to Shanghai in early 1947 and did testify at the trials of Colonel Matsuda and the Mukden POW camp doctor, Captain Kuwashima. Boylan also pointed out that if no action was taken against Hankins, the file of complaints about him would not have been retained by the Judge Advocate General's Office. William Cunliffe, a senior archivist at the National Archives, confirmed that the postwar priority for war crimes prosecutors would surely be focused on brutality by the captors, not lack of leadership on the part of a POW officer.[19]

Despite his postwar advance in rank to lieutenant colonel and his avoidance of court-martial proceedings, Stanley Hankins died within five years of the war's end from the prolonged effects of acute alcohol poisoning.

8

Escape

On April 1, 1943, the Japanese commander ordered all Mukden prisoners to turn in their winter clothing, despite the fact that the weather was still very cold. Two American Marines, Sgt. Joe Bill Chastain and Cpl. Victor Paliotto, failed to turn in their warm clothing and were immediately accused of planning to escape—which, in fact, they were. The two were put into an unheated guard-house cell and given no blankets. According to many Mukden survivors who had endured time in the guard house, the confined men had to jump up and down all night to keep from freezing to death. Chastain and Paliotto were not allowed to sleep in the daytime.

"During this period they implicated a third man [not named] who was promptly confined with them," Lt. William Thompson notes in his history of the camp. "They proclaimed their innocence for about a week, but the strain was too much. They decided to talk after the Japanese had promised them blankets for a confession. They told a story of how they had planned to climb over the fence at the west side of the camp, cross the fields to the railway, catch a freight train northward as far as possible, and make their way to Siberia. The Japanese, pleased to think they had prevented an outbreak, forgave the men, released one [unnamed], gave the other two their blankets, and sentenced them to one [additional] month's confinement in the guard house."[1] A rumor circulated in the camp that upon hearing of the men's confession of their planned escape, Maj. Stanley Hankins, who was known for his dislike of Marines, said, "If it were up to me, those men would be shot." Hankins never lived down that rumor, whether or not he actually made the comment.

It was May before Chastain and Paliotto were released, but they immediately began trying to rebuild their strength. Pfc. Oliver Allen, who worked in the camp kitchen with Chastain, said the sergeant lifted rocks. "He was one of those guys who couldn't stand confinement. He couldn't take it."[2]

Although Sergeant Chastain and Corporal Paliotto were put in separate barracks after their release from the guard house, they managed to recruit a third

POW, S1c Ferdinand "Freddie" Meringolo, a crew member of the submarine tender USS *Canopus*, for their plans. Over the next several weeks, the three made careful, detailed preparations for their escape as the weather gradually warmed. Chastain discovered a textbook on a bench at the MKK factory, left there by a Japanese intern from a vocational school. Inside he found a fold-out map of China and tore it out. Decun Gao, a Manchurian factory foreman, was accused by the student of ripping out the map. Gao knew that one of the POWs had stolen the map, but he didn't know which one or why the map was wanted. Gao went to a street stand the next day and bought a replacement map for the student, thinking that would be the end of the incident.[3]

Meanwhile, Chastain asked Paliotto to hide the map, which he did by removing a piece of baseboard in the factory bathroom and concealing the map behind it. At the factory kitchen Chastain stole two fish knives, concealing them in his shoes as he walked back to camp and hiding them "somewhere" in the camp. The three planners managed to steal a magnet and use it to make a crude compass, and they acquired some dried dog meat for their trip.

On the night of June 21, 1943, the three POWs made their escape. The next morning, when the men were discovered missing at *tenko* (roll call), Colonel Matsuda ordered several measures of punishment for the American prisoners, implying that they all shared blame for this infuriating and embarrassing insult to his command. Two days after the discovery, Matsuda sent a report to the POW Information Bureau in Tokyo announcing that the escape had occurred.

For an entire week the American prisoners were confined to their barracks and made to sit in upright positions, at attention, with their legs crossed. Sgt. Thomas Bullock stated in a postwar affidavit: "After having been in this position for several hours, I yawned and stretched back, and the Japanese civilian guard, referred to by us as 'the Wolf,' saw me stretch and yawn, and walked up to me and beat me severely with a book. I had taken off my glasses before he beat me, and when he finished I put them back on again. This apparently enraged him, because he came back and began to beat me again until he had broken my glasses. The 'Wolf' . . . had a ferocious expression on his face, and actually looked like a wolf."[4]

Sgt. Thomas Proulx added, "The food ration for the entire camp was cut considerably. Furthermore, the men in the same barrack as the men who escaped were forced to sit at attention every day for three weeks as punishment."[5] Cpl. Robert Wolfersberger recalled, "Our captors had set up a night 'fire guard,' and he was instructed to report any empty bed-bunks. I was one of about six 'fire guards' on duty the night the escape was attempted and we were therefore guilty of negligence and spent thirty days in a darkened, unlit cell with only bread and water, except a bowl of beans or maize every third day. No talking between prisoners was allowed and one canteen of water and one sourdough bun a day was the ration. The dark loneliness was very depressing and didn't build any favorable attitudes toward our captors."[6]

In his narrative history Lieutenant Thompson added details to the night of the escape and the retaliatory punishments that followed:

The night of 21 June was quiet and very dark until about 11 P.M., when a bright moon came up. Before going to bed, Doctor Shabart remarked, "What a night for an escape." Just how prophetic his words were was shown next morning at TENKO (roll call) when three Barracks Leaders breathlessly rushed up to report that one man from each of their barracks had disappeared during the night. Two of the men were of the three who had been confined for attempting to escape, the third was a man not previously suspected. Lieutenant Yamaura, Supply Officer, nicknamed "Chester" by the men, was officer-of-the-day. When the report was made to him he gulped, blushed, stuttered, and ran out of camp to report to the commander without bothering to complete the roll call. Later, the guard around camp was strengthened, squads of guards armed with rifles and fixed bayonets double-timed about the area inspecting fences for possible means of escape. The "Bull" appeared on horseback. All prisoners were ordered to remain inside barracks while a careful count was made, and then were ordered to remain inside for the rest of the day while all available Japanese personnel were organized to scour the country for the "absconders," as the three men were called by the Japanese. There was no factory work for the day, but late in the afternoon the Japanese allowed a small detail to go to the cemetery to plant flowers. This detail was under guard of a single officer with an empty rifle.

On the 23rd, the factory men went to work, with the exception of the men in the three barracks of the escapers. These men remained in their barracks to be questioned by the Japanese who were anxious to find anyone who had aided the escape or failed in his "duty" to report the affair earlier. Previous to this time the Japanese had ordered the prisoners to organize and maintain night guards, whose duty was to remain awake in one-hour shifts during the sleeping hours and report all unusual matters, particularly fires and escapes. Consequently the night guards on duty that night and the Barracks Leaders of those three barracks were under particular observation and investigation by the Japanese. The next day the Japanese issued orders that security groups of ten men would be formed immediately and that all men of the group would be held responsible and punished if one member of the group escaped. Also, the night guards on duty at the time of the escape would be regarded as accomplices and punished accordingly if they failed to report such an escape immediately.

On the 24th, a rope was strung about three feet above the ground and at a distance of never less than ten feet from the barbed-wire fence. Prisoners were prohibited on penalty of death from crossing over that rope. It invoked even additional hardships as it cut off from use a large area at the front of the camp, the camp's coal supply used for cooking, the kitchen's garbage pit, the drying racks of one barrack, and the latrine of another [barrack]. Men in this latter had to "double up" in the use of the latrine of their nearest neighbor. Also, the Japanese announced this day that anyone leaving the barracks between the hours of 8:30 P.M. and 6:00 A.M., except for the purpose of going to the latrine, would be shot. By the 28th, the investigation and trials had been completed and the Japanese announced that all men in the three "escape" barracks would sit at the foot of their bunks at attention for seven days, being allowed only to go to the latrine but not to smoke; all night guards on duty the night of the 21st would be sentenced to ten days' "heavy" confinement in the guard house (this meant a man would have only two blankets and receive regular food only every third day, on the two intervening days he had a canteen of cold water and a bun for each meal); two of the Barracks Leaders were sentenced to seven days' confinement; the other barracks leader was given thirty days' confinement because he slept in the same room as one of the missing; and that the entire camp would be prohibited all forms of amusement and recreation for an indefinite period.

The camp authorities, no doubt, lost much "face" over this escape. In order to justify themselves, they placed the blame on all the remaining prisoners and meted out the above punishments to all men even remotely connected with the three escapees. From that day on the attitude of the Japanese toward the prisoners was notably changed.[7] But amid all the retaliation, the prisoners had one benefit from the escape: a very stepped-up timetable to move them to the new camp compound, with its fourteen-foot brick wall topped by electrified barbed wire. The move took place on July 29, 1943.

The day after the escape was discovered, June 21, 1943, Maj. Robert Peaty made an entry in his diary: "Personally, I hope the men get through and can make known the scandal of the lack of medical care which was responsible for the deaths of fifteen percent of the American prisoners of war in this camp." In a detailed report to Tokyo, Colonel Matsuda noted:

> The fact, however, that we failed to discover earlier the maps and knives obtained from the factory had facilitated their escape. . . . Although security and surveillance measures are being taken in the usual strict manner, a more strict security measure will be adopted considering their psychological factor. [He was aware of the POWs' resentment that those not directly involved were being made to pay such a high price.] Those who are suspected of being the most liable to escape are confined to the guardhouse and who at the same time, Marine noncommissioned officers and others require close watch, are being checked for their presence during the night by night patrol officers. The personnel on night duty are checking and recording the names of those who go to the latrine after lights out and others who are on official duty. . . . In short, it is logical to assume that everyone has an intention to escape in view of improved physical condition and previous training. Camp personnel are, therefore, determined to do their utmost to prevent recurrence of any such incident in the future.[8]

But perhaps the most severe and tragic punishment for the escape was handed out to Manchurian factory worker Decun Gao. Because he had replaced the stolen map from the Japanese student's textbook, he was arrested, tortured, and

POW cemetery, Mukden, 1945. Photo by Joseph A. Vater.

sentenced to ten years in prison. His wife had just given birth to a baby boy, and with no source of income for her and the child, the baby died of starvation. Sixty years later Gao was still cursing the Japanese.[9]

Meanwhile, the three escapees, in a remarkable odyssey, traveled northwest three hundred kilometers in eleven days. Later they described their journey in detail to their captors:

> On the night of 21 June, after lights out, they went to the latrine, gathered their articles, and assembled at a hollow place inside the compound, on the east side of the warehouse located on the north side of the dispensary barracks. No. 516 [Chastain] acted as the scout leader and waited for the opportune time. The time was approximately 22 hours 21 June. It required between 40 minutes and one hour to get close to the barbed wire fence by crawling, while paying attention to the bark of the dogs. It took about one or two minutes to get through the fence and, fearing pursuit by the military dogs, they took to the same road they used to pass every day for work.
>
> After the escape, they headed for Outer Mongolia, by-passing the villages. They continued their flight by stealing from the fields and by means of a map and compass. But when they entered Hsingan Hansheng, they failed to find any farm crops in the fields. They were forced to enter the village. They explained to the natives, "We are Germans, we were on the way back to Germany from Japan, when our plane crashed. Three other crew members have died and after burying them, we came this far on foot. Give us food." They explained this with pantomime gestures to which the villagers responded with welcome. They went into another village [Liang Jiazi] and did the same thing as before, it aroused the suspicion of a Mongolian policeman [Sofu Tokugawara] who insisted on going to the scene of the crash to look over the situation. He mounted his horse and departed with two villagers [Baku Tian and Gao Fengshan]. Thereupon the three escapees decided that escape would be impossible unless these three Mongolians were killed. Thus, when they

came to a hollow area in front of a sand dune, the three POWs simultaneously jumped on the three Mongolians. Number 516 [Chastain] stabbed the policeman to death, number 1125 [Meringolo] stabbed one of the villagers [Baku], but his flimsy knife failed to kill the villager and number 516 came to his aid and stabbed [the villager] in the neck. In the meantime, number 444 [Paliotto] fought the remaining Mongolian [Gao] near the horse but the Mongolian got away to inform the villagers.

The three POWs thought it was best to run away from the scene and took cover in a thicket. Later, they were discovered by their footprints on the sand and were surrounded by the villagers. After a struggle Number 1125 and number 444 were felled and wounded, and number 516 raised his hands to surrender. They were all captured by the villagers. Two of the villagers were wounded.

The above information was obtained by actually investigating the spot and hearing the testimony after the prisoners were captured and sent back to Mukden. The offenders, however, seemed to have resigned themselves to the fact and readily confessed.[10] [This is a vast understatement; the three POWs were beaten and tortured for a prolonged period before confessing these details.]

Lieutenant Thompson described the return of the three escapees to the Mukden camp on July 6, 1943:

The three who had escaped fifteen days before were brought back into camp for about an hour, a sorry sight to the other prisoners who were not allowed to approach or signal to them. A technical sergeant, [Chastain] thought to be the leader, was handcuffed; the other two had their hands bound behind their backs with rope. All three were barefoot. The sergeant looked a little thin, but otherwise not too bad. The second looked sick and most of the back of his coveralls was stained with blood. The third one's clothes were much blood stained, his head was covered by a huge bandage, and his face was thin and yellow. All were dressed in American Army uniforms and coveralls. Accompanied by a large group of Japanese officers and soldiers, the men were forced to show their route and means of escape. Evidently, they had crawled along a ditch and under the barbed wire where it was about two feet above the ditch. After showing this, they were taken away without having had a chance to communicate with other prisoners. Later in the day, Corporal Noda, interpreter, released the information in the camp that the men were being held for military trial and punishment and that they would probably go to the capital, Hsinking, for the trial. He also told the story that the escapers had been captured by Manchu police and had received their wounds at that time by resisting capture. Turned over to Japanese military authorities, they had been given treatment, care and rest before being interrogated. He said that they had been asked if they wanted to give any message to the men in the camp and they had written a note saying it was no good to escape as the going was too rough on the outside.[11]

Other prisoners remembered that the three escapees were made to stand barefoot in ashes and proclaim to their assembled fellow POWs that escape should not be attempted. After that they were severely beaten, and the POWs were made to watch. RM1c Randall Edwards, USN, recalled the horror of those beatings: "They were beaten so badly in front of all of us that I wouldn't be surprised if they were already dead right there, they were beaten so badly. They were probably already dead before they were executed."[12]

Lieutenant Thompson elaborated on the steps Colonel Matsuda mentioned taking to prevent further escapes:

> In escaping, these men had taken with them salt, sugar, canned food [purchased through the canteen], bread, and some rough maps of the country traced on drawing paper obtained at the factory. The Japanese soon issued orders prohibiting individual possession of these articles. No drawing or writing paper was allowed. The privilege of buying canned goods was discontinued [for the enlisted men; on July 13 the officers were allowed to make food purchases for their officers' mess]. The camp's issue of sugar was reduced. Men were ordered to eat their bread at the meal for which it was issued. Periodic "shakedown" inspections were made from then on by the Japanese, and men found having any of these articles among their possessions were questioned and often punished.[13]

The trial of the three prisoners, which took place on July 30, was conducted in Japanese and lasted half an hour. The sentence was death. It is worth noting that the men were given the death sentence not just for escaping but also for murdering the Mongolian policeman and attempting to murder the other two villagers.

A year later, after their deaths were confirmed by the Japanese government to the Swiss government and relayed to American officials, it was announced in the American press. As reported in the *New York Times*, a spokesman for the State Department told reporters that if a prisoner escaped in the United States from a prison camp and killed another person in the process of escape, the prisoner would be subject to court-martial and possible execution under international law.[14]

The July 31, 1943, execution of Sergeant Chastain, Corporal Paliotto, and Seaman Meringolo was described in graphic detail by Lieutenant Miki, who witnessed the execution. His description was entered into the 1947 Shanghai trial transcript:

> The faces of the three men were covered with white cloths and then blindfolds of white cloth was placed over their eyes. Their wrists were tied to the arms of wooden crosses and they were made to sit down folding their legs. The riflemen took kneeling positions seven or eight meters away from the men, one man aiming at the forehead and another at the heart of each of the three men. The commander of the execution squad gave the order and six shots were fired at one time. A small quantity of blood spurted out from the white cloths covering the faces of the men and from the chest sections of the overalls the men wore. After the medical captain that had been sent by the Kwantung

Army had examined them, the corpses were delivered to the camp. We placed them in a coffin [but not before a Japanese soldier ripped the gold cross from Seaman Meringolo's neck], and buried them in the war prisoners' cemetery [in unmarked graves.] I remember clearly a non-commissioned officer of the army prison offering some beautiful wild flowers to the dead as we were about to bury them, saying: "There is no guilt after death so go peacefully to your place in Heaven."[15]

WO1 Arnold Bocksel said he was standing next to Major Hankins as the three men were being buried and that Hankins had tears rolling down his cheeks. Their fellow prisoners did not, however, react peacefully to the executions. Cpl. Joseph Petak summed up their attitude, stating that the "effect of the executions left a mark on us. We became vindictive, vengeful and surly. We became uncooperative at the factory and slowed down the work tremendously. Sabotage increased tenfold. Sabotage went on a rampage. No one could accept the punishment as being justified."[16] Perhaps it's just as well the prisoners at Mukden did not have access to the *New York Times*.

The three escapees: Sgt. Joe Bill Chastain, USMC; Cpl. Victor Paliotto, USMC; and S1c Ferdinand Meringolo, USN. Photos supplied by Chastain, Paliotto, and Meringolo families

Despite the detailed report Colonel Matsuda filed with the POW Information Bureau in Tokyo in August 1943, the Japanese government did not inform the Swiss ambassador stationed in Tokyo, Camille Gorgé, who was representing American interests, or the International Committee of the Red Cross, which was Japan's obligation under international law, about the executions. Nor did the Japanese government follow protocol in passing on the death certificates for the three prisoners, which had been duly recorded and filed in Tokyo. It was not until ICRC representative Max Pestalozzi visited the Mukden camp in November 1943 that Matsuda thought to mention the executions to him. But Pestalozzi became ill upon his return to Geneva and delayed filing his report until late December 1943. The Swiss government did not notify the American legation in Bern until

January 1944. The American Legation immediately asked the Swiss government to obtain confirmation of the executions from the Japanese government, but that confirmation was not received by American diplomats until June 27, 1944, and it was only then that the American government took steps to officially notify the families of the men.

On July 28, 1944, the Navy Department sent a letter to the Meringolo family notifying them of their son's death on July 31, 1943, noting that the delay in notification was due to the slow response from the Japanese government. But the Meringolo family was furious in their grief, according to Meringolo's sister Catherine, and the family complained loudly to the press, accusing the Navy of choosing to withhold the information. Catherine Meringolo Quoma added that her father was "heartbroken that he had signed Freddie into the Navy" and that news of her brother's execution had hastened her mother's death.[17]

Sergeant Chastain's father, Sterling, told the Associated Press from his home in Waco, Texas, that he received the news of his son's death from the Red Cross on July 31, 1944, exactly a year after it had occurred. And Corporal Paliotto's mother, Julia, when contacted at her home in Cranston, Rhode Island, was quoted as saying, "The only thing we can do for Victor is to pray for him. He did his best but I hope his brother who is with the American forces in Italy does not have to pay so great a price."[18] The Paliotto family was notified by the Marine Corps about the execution of their son; the letter gave details about where the bullets had entered his body. His remains were not returned until February 1948. Corporal Paliotto is buried in St. Ann's cemetery in Cranston.[19] Seaman Meringolo is buried in Pinelawn National Cemetery on Long Island, New York.

Chinese historian Jing Yang has added a poignant footnote to the story of the three Mukden escapees. Yang, a native of Shenyang (Mukden), set out in May 2005 to locate the little Inner Mongolian village of Liang Jiazi, where the three men were recaptured and turned over to the Japanese. Yang did find the village, and he found Yinshan Wang, a sixty-nine-year-old villager who remembered seeing the three strangers as a six-year-old boy. He showed Yang the thicket where the men had taken refuge before the villagers smoked them out, saying that the villagers still call the spot the "American Hump." "What happened to them?" Wang asked historian Yang. When told they were executed, Wang, saddened, said ruefully, "If only we had known they were Americans, we might have let them go. We thought they were spies."[20]

9

Red Cross Double-Crossed

One of the cruelest policies of the Japanese government during the Pacific war, a policy even the Nazis did not observe, was to deny Red Cross aid to the POWs. Red Cross representatives were not allowed access to POW camps or civilian internment camps, the Japanese refused to distribute Red Cross parcels that actually had been delivered to these camps, and they blocked relief funds that had been made available by both private agencies and Allied governments for the benefit of prisoners in Japanese captivity.

This latter, most egregious act came about when the Japanese government agreed in August 1944 to sign an elaborate written arrangement crafted by the International Committee of the Red Cross, the Swiss National Bank, and American, British, and Dutch treasury representatives. The agreement was to allow the ICRC to deposit prisoner relief funds donated by the United States, Britain, and the Netherlands into special accounts maintained by the Swiss National Bank, to which ICRC representatives would have access at the bank's many branches throughout Japan and Japanese-occupied Asia. But at the last minute the Japanese government changed its mind (eyeing the lucrative exchange rate and wishing to profit from it), insisting that the deposits be made in the Yokohama Specie Bank and pledging that the Japanese government would see to their prompt deployment. Having no choice, and not wishing to delay an agreement that had taken nearly a year to negotiate, the Swiss reluctantly acquiesced. But in a classic double-cross, once Japan had control of the relief funds, the government ordered the Yokohama Specie Bank not to release the funds. And there the funds sat, gaining interest for the rest of the war, while prisoners starved and lacked clothing, while POW physicians went without lifesaving medicines and surgical instruments, and while frustrated Red Cross workers complained to their representatives throughout Asia and Geneva—to no avail.

Japan's obligation under the 1929 Geneva Conventions is widely misunderstood. The Conventions, or series of meetings, which took place in Geneva, Switzerland, over a period of many months were tasked with reviewing the conduct of governments during wartime, had last been revised in 1907 prior to World War I, and were intended to correct breaches that had occurred, such as the use of nerve gas. While it is true that the Japanese Diet (parliament) had refused to ratify the convention its delegate had signed in Geneva regarding the treatment of prisoners of war (arguing that no other nation would be concerned with Japanese POWs, since Japan's military personnel were taught not to surrender but to kill themselves in preference to such dishonor), the Diet did in fact ratify the Geneva Convention with reference to cooperating with the Red Cross—a fact often overlooked by historians, memoirists, and scholars.

Thus the government of Japan had, since 1929, committed itself to abiding by the principles set forth by the International Committee of the Red Cross and to recognizing the legitimacy of ICRC requests to visit prison camps, to provide lists of captives, to meet with officials, and to distribute relief supplies delivered by ICRC representatives. By barring access to Red Cross representatives, holding up relief funds, and ignoring repeated requests by Swiss diplomats representing American and British interests, the Japanese government, as well as prison camp commanders, were guilty of a classic double-cross throughout the Pacific war. And the impact on the prisoners at Mukden—along with captives in Japanese custody everywhere else—was enormous.

Ten days after Japan's attack on Pearl Harbor, Secretary of State Cordell Hull urgently asked our Swiss diplomatic representatives to assure the Japanese government that the United States intended to honor both the Red Cross and POW provisions of the 1929 Geneva Conventions and wished to hear what the Japanese government's intentions were. Seven anxious weeks later, Japan replied that it was "strictly observing Geneva Red Cross Convention as a signatory state. . . . Although not bound by the Convention relative [to] treatment of prisoners of war Japan will apply *mutatis mutandis* provisions of that convention to American prisoners of war in its power." The phrase "mutatis mutandis" was clarified by Japan's foreign minister Shigenori Togo to mean, in essence, "as long as observing the convention didn't interfere with Japan's laws in force."[1]

The first information American officials received about our prisoners in Mukden came on July 3, 1943, nearly seven months after the POWs had stumbled into their makeshift camp in that frozen location. A cablegram had been sent the previous day from the ICRC's delegate in Tokyo, Frederick Pavaracini, to Geneva, and forwarded to the ICRC delegation in the United States. The cable transmitted a report from the Japanese Prisoner of War Information Bureau, confirming just 804 American POWs listed as being there. It quotes the cryptic Japanese report: "Health improving. Patients in hospital fifteen. Second germ examination [the second visit by the Unit 731 medical team] April sixteenth of 1461 POW revealed two cases infectious diseases including above. Special preventive measure against infectious diseases taken. Light patients about 100. Weight increasing. Serving special foods excepting medicinal herbs for patients discontinued after April eleventh owing better health conditions. Canteen established, pigs raised. POW want Japanese dictionaries [to] selfstudy Japanese language, books etc. Mails sent 390, received few."[2]

Later that same month three American POWs at Mukden would be executed, but that information was not transmitted until the following December, after an ICRC representative was finally allowed to visit the Mukden camp, following repeated requests from the United States, Geneva, and POW camp leaders in Mukden.

However, the first eyewitness reports Allied officials received about the increasingly desperate plight of our POWs in Japanese captivity came not from ICRC representatives but from young Thai students trained in the United States by the Office of Strategic Services and spirited back into Thailand with instructions to position themselves along the jungle paths of the infamous Burma Railway, then being constructed at great human cost by British, Australian, American, and Dutch POWs. By late 1943 Thai observers were reporting the emaciated condition, lack of food and medicine, and extremely high death rate among the Allied POWs. A November 11, 1943, diary entry by Australian Lt. Col. J. M. Williams, commander of the Allied advance work force on the railway, summed up the POWs' desperate situation: "We are completely out of foodstuffs. No meals can be served today."[3]

By early 1944 it became apparent to Allied governments that they had to find some way to get more relief supplies to POWs in Japanese custody everywhere. On February 11, 1944, Under Secretary of State Edward Stettinius sent a telegram full of barely concealed frustration to the Swiss legation in Tokyo listing twenty prior messages dating back to July 1942 citing mistreatment of POWs to which the Japanese had not replied. Stettinius' frustration was fueled by a February 5, 1944, Japanese news report quoting Sadao Iguchi, spokesman for Japan's Prisoner of War Information Bureau, claiming that "Japan is leaving no stone unturned to carry out all possible humanitarian measures in connection with her treatment of prisoners of war, that the mutual countries concerned, the Vatican and the International Committee of the Red Cross are aware of the Japanese policy and . . . the treatment of prisoners of war and civilian internees in Japanese hands is fair and considerate."[4] By the day of Iguchi's statement, 212 Americans who had died from disease, malnutrition, lack of medical care, and exposure to extreme cold lay buried in the cemetery outside the Mukden POW camp—and liberation was still a year and a half away.

Clearly a way around Japan's inability or unwillingness to provide for POWs, and its denials of this fact, had to be found. The only hope seemed to be to vastly supplement the resources of the ICRC and to provide the organization's representatives with more funds to purchase supplies for delivery to POW camps. So the American, British, and Dutch treasuries set up special accounts in the Swiss National Bank to deposit funds upon which ICRC representatives could draw as needed. In April 1944 the U.S. Treasury arranged to use the already existing "Swiss National Bank Special Account T'" through the Federal Reserve Bank of New York as a repository for this super-secret relief fund. But arrangements to deposit money into this account took many more months to complete, while POWs died daily throughout Asia. Finally, on August 17, 1944 (exactly one year before the Mukden POWs were freed by an American OSS team), a clearing agreement for the Allied government relief fund was settled among the governments of the United States, Britain, Sweden (representing the Netherlands), Switzerland, and Japan. But, as mentioned earlier, instead of allowing the Swiss National Bank to deposit the Allied relief money in its Asian branches, the Japanese government insisted that the Swiss Bank deposit the money in Japan's Yokohama Specie Bank, pledging that distribution would be promptly made. Despite the urgent pleas of Red Cross officials, Swiss diplomats could not pry those funds from the Yokohama Specie Bank, which had been ordered by the Japanese government to delay their release.

Barely a month after the relief fund agreement was signed, an event that dramatically illustrated the urgent need for these funds occurred. On September 12, 1944, a Japanese merchant ship carrying mostly Australian POWs northward from the now-completed Burma Railway to Japan for further use as slave laborers at Japanese factories, mines, shipyards, and steel mills was sunk by a U.S. submarine, whose captain and crew were unaware of the ship's Allied human cargo. Three days later, that same submarine, the *Pampanito,* circled back and rescued 157 survivors. The stories they told, secretly, to Australian authorities shocked and horrified the governments of Australia, Britain, and the United States, which debated for weeks whether to make these confirmed Japanese atrocities public.

Meanwhile, on October 6, 1944, the Swiss chargé d'affaires in Bangkok, a Mr. Siegenthaler, sent a cryptic message to Bern: "Funds are exhausted. Please speed up remittance. [Today] I cabled [Swiss Ambassador to Tokyo Camille] Gorgé: 'On 19 September the Department authorized a transfer of 500,000 [Swiss francs] for me via Tokyo for the relief program for war prisoners. Because of exhausted cash funds I have to discontinue the program. I therefore request intercession with Japanese authorities so that transfer will be speeded up.'"[5] As legislatures and consulates exchanged news of the secret Allied government relief agreement, Japan's foreign minister, Mamoru Shigemitsu, began getting queries from his field offices. On November 13, 1944, he spelled out the arrangements of the agreement in a secret detailed reply to his ministry in Saigon, ending the message with these words: "The details of this agreement are secret from all but the officials concerned and care is to be taken that they do not leak out. Care should also be taken that the working of this agreement is not hampered by delays in paying."[6] Apparently Japan's foreign minister was unaware of his own government's instructions to its central bank.

Six days later, on November 19, 1944, President Franklin Roosevelt, Prime Minister Winston Churchill, and F. M. Forde, the Australian acting prime minister, made simultaneous speeches to their elected officials, detailing the mistreatment, high death rates, and starvation to which prisoners in Japanese custody were being subjected and putting the government of Japan on notice that it would be held accountable for these war crimes.

Possibly in retaliation for these public disclosures by the Allied heads of state, which were globally reported in the press, the Japanese government, in a move even the Nazis didn't have the nerve to make, cut off communications in late 1944 between the ICRC headquarters in Geneva and its officials in Asia. As a result no one knew for sure until after the war how few relief supplies intended for POWs actually reached them. Japan's double-cross of the Red Cross remained a wartime secret.

The Mukden POW camp was no exception to this double-cross; in fact, prisoners there were victims of it long before the 1944 Allied relief fund was set in place. Because the Mukden camp was one of the first ones established (October 1942), and because it was one of the largest, relief organizations were immediately aware that extra help would be needed by prisoners isolated in such a harsh climate. On January 30, 1943, Colonel Matsuda announced that the Vatican had donated 1,500 yen for the relief of the American prisoners at Mukden. Immediately Major Hankins requested that this money be used for food and desperately needed medical supplies, but Colonel Matsuda denied this request. The Japanese, he said, would supply food and medicine themselves; the Vatican money should be used for recreational purposes.[7]

Matsuda's denial of Hankins' urgent request, and the reason he gave for it, highlights the long-entrenched Japanese desires to "save face" and refrain from accepting a gift that makes the recipient beholden to the giver. Allowing the Vatican money to be spent for food and medicine would be an admission to the world that the Japanese were not able—or willing—to supply adequate food and medicine to their prisoners. Musical instruments and recreational equipment could be seen as supplemental, not necessary, items.

The stockpiling of Red Cross boxes delivered to Mukden as well as POW camps in many locations was, in a bizarre way, another manifestation of such entrenched Japanese mind-sets. POWs at Mitsui's Omuta coal-mine complex in Fukuoka, Japan, discovered upon liberation in August 1945 not only Red Cross boxes withheld from them during World War II but also earlier Red Cross boxes donated after the devastating earthquake that rocked Japan in 1923. The disintegrated boxes had been locked up, undisturbed, for more than two decades because the Japanese government did not want to admit that it could not meet its own people's needs. The Japanese government reacted in a similar way when a huge earthquake caused widespread devastation in the area of Kobe, Japan, in January 1995. Worldwide offers of aid were politely refused, while the citizens of Kobe were seen on TV complaining about how slowly their government was moving to help them. In 1995 some determined relief workers arrived on the scene and just did what they could. But the prisoners at Mukden had no intercessors in the brutally harsh winter of 1942–43.

So despite the pleas of the senior American POW officer, Colonel Matsuda notified the Vatican that it was welcome to use its funds to purchase musical instruments and recreational equipment for the Allied prisoners. On March 27, 1943, the Vatican gifts arrived, and the hungry, freezing, sick prisoners were given two guitars, two mandolins, two violins and six harmonicas—to be used only on Sundays. When a British officer was caught playing an accordion on a weekday, the musical instruments were taken away for a month as punishment for this infraction of the rules.[8] (Major Hankins, apparently a skilled craftsman, used materials to create a cello, which is on display at the Smithsonian Museum in Washington, D.C.)

The trouble was that food at Mukden remained inadequate and virtually no medicines were forthcoming—except a few items one kind Japanese camp doctor, Juro Oki, managed to acquire and paid for out of his own pocket. (Oki may have been merely a medical orderly, but his kindness has been mentioned by many Mukden survivors in their depositions for war crimes investigations, interviews, and memoirs.) The Mukden POW doctors, like POW camp doctors everywhere in the Pacific, were furious to discover quantities of medical supplies and surgical instruments upon liberation in August 1945, when they finally gained access to the locked warehouses within the camp where stacks of more than three hundred Red Cross boxes were stored.

However, the Mukden camp had the unique distinction of receiving three visits by Red Cross officials in the nearly three years of its existence. (The Japanese denied ICRC representatives access to most camp locations, saying they were in a "war zone.") After repeated requests by Major Peaty and Major Hankins, as well as continual protests by American and International Red Cross officials, Colonel Matsuda and his superiors in Tokyo perhaps realized that their repeated refusals might get them in trouble one day, so in November 1943, a team of ICRC delegates was finally given permission to visit the camp.

On November 13, 1943, ICRC delegate Max Pestalozzi arrived at the Mukden camp. It was a very controlled occasion. Only British senior officer Major Peaty, American senior officer Major Hankins, and five American enlisted men were allowed to see Pestalozzi—in the presence of the entire Japanese staff. Peaty described the visit in his diary: "A short interview was permitted in the presence of the entire Japanese staff, during which we were able to report that there had been no previous contact with the Red Cross. Major Hankins and about five of the American enlisted men were present. His [Pestalozzi's] questions and our replies were all translated to the Japanese. As regards treatment, I said that I thought that the basic policy of the central authorities in Tokio [sic] appeared to be reasonable, but that the local administration of it left a lot to be desired."[9] Whether Peaty's remarks were fully translated for his Japanese captors is unknown. Only he and Hankins were allowed to speak; the enlisted men had to remain silent.

Mukden POW Lt. William Thompson, in writing his narrative of life at Mukden following liberation, also noted Pestalozzi's visit:

> He was hurried through the camp and allowed very little conversation with the prisoners. After the inspection, he was allowed to talk with the American leader [Hankins], the British leader [Peaty], and one or two selected enlisted men [who were not allowed to speak]. At this time, he said the prisoners could expect mail and parcels in the near future. This Red Cross inspection was preceded by several days of intense effort on the part of the Japanese to have the camp put on an excellent appearance. Even the grounds were swept with long brush brooms. The following day, the Japanese Propaganda Corps appeared in camp with many cameras. They took numerous movies and still shots and took recordings for a broadcast.[10]

Apparently Pestalozzi knew that he was getting guarded answers from the POWs, but the report he wrote gave the impression that everything was satisfactory at Mukden. Writing of the new barracks to which the prisoners had been moved the previous July, he noted:

> The barracks, or quarters for the prisoners are of brick and newly built. They contain electric lights and heat. Ventilation is satisfactory. . . . Each prisoner has one mattress, six army blankets, two sheets, one pillow and one pillow case. In summer they are issued mosquito nets. The officers and men have separate sections. Sanitary facilities . . . are connected to the barrack buildings. Privates and non-commissioned officers are allowed a hot bath every other day, and officers every day. The prisoners have three meals a day which consist of bread, vegetables, some fruits and some meats or fish occasionally. . . . Each man is allowed four cigarettes per day. Officers ten more. Preventative measures are taken against diseases. The Red Cross hospital and Kwantung Army headquarters and general hospital take care of the ill prisoners efficiently. There are: one Japanese Army surgeon, 6 medical orderlies, all Japanese, besides four Prisoner of War Army surgeons and twenty-nine orderlies from the prisoners.
>
> Officer prisoners receive the same pay as officers in the Japanese Army and are not required to work. Other prisoners receive pay for work which consists of maintenance of the camp and administrative work. Others work in the camp work-shops, mending and doing general utility work. The prisoners for this camp have a large sports ground with separate spaces for volley-ball and basket-ball. They also have a foot-ball field and base-ball diamond. Indoor games are available as are gramophones and newspapers. Officers may write

three letters and three post cards per year, NCOs four cards and Privates three cards per year.

So far, no distribution of relief goods from the Red Cross has been made. Otherwise, this camp makes a satisfactory impression. The prisoners have no complaints to make as to the treatment and state that conditions are better than they expected.[11]

What a rosy picture the ICRC's Pestalozzi described! Apparently he got most of his information from the camp commandant, Colonel Matsuda. Peaty noted in his secret diary that both he and Hankins were very guarded in their remarks. Even so, they were unsure how accurately their comments were translated to the Swiss representative and all their comments were made in the presence of the entire Japanese officer staff of the camp.

Matsuda neglected to mention that the barracks were rife with fleas and other vermin; that canteen items were virtually nonexistent; that there was almost no medicine available to treat the prisoners, except what Oki purchased out of his own pocket or what Pfc. Robert Brown, the American orderly, was able to purloin after he stole the key to the Japanese supply room; that the "general utility work" often consisted of war work (contrary to international law); that the prisoners were given no safety equipment, goggles, or gloves when they did work such as welding in the "work-shops"; that POWs were allowed almost no time to pursue recreational activities with the restricted and nearly nonexistent sporting equipment; that they were not allowed to use musical equipment except on Sundays (and this privilege was often suspended for minor infractions of rules); and that the prisoners' families hardly ever received the mail supposedly sent from this camp. Pestalozzi did note that the U.S. POWs had received no mail since May 1942, after the fall of the last outpost in the Philippines, Corregidor.

It is interesting to note that Pestalozzi slipped in just one line about the lack of distribution of Red Cross parcels yet noted that the Vatican had sent "yen 1500 which had been used to buy musical equipment, clocks and other smaller items," according, of course, to Colonel Matsuda.

Matsuda listed 154 POW deaths at the camp, 62 "en route" (on board the hellships at sea), and 6 at Pusan (too ill to travel). He failed to note that virtually all the POWs who had died were Americans, and that most had died from pneumonia, exposure, starvation, and untreated diseases associated with malnutrition. He also underreported the deaths at Pusan; there were 48.

But Pestalozzi's report contained one bombshell, near the end, under the heading of "Courts Martial": "Three were sentenced to death for murder and attempted escape." When his report was filed at ICRC headquarters in Geneva on December 15, 1943, it provoked an immediate inquiry from the ICRC to Tokyo and an urgent request from the United States for details. The Japanese did not supply those details about the escape, recapture, military trial, and July 31,

1943, execution of American POWs Sergeant Chastain, Seaman Meringolo, and Corporal Paliotto until June 1944, so the families were not notified until a year later that their sons had been executed by the Japanese.

Whether Pestalozzi knew that the Swedish relief ship *Gripsholm* was steaming toward Tokyo (arriving December 14, 1943, with mail and packages for POW camps, including Mukden) cannot be ascertained, but within weeks of his visit, in early January 1944, the first packages from home were received at Mukden. Thompson recorded that the "Japanese received about fourteen of these packages each day. Before a prisoner could receive his package, it was entirely unwrapped and inspected by a Japanese officer and all wrapping material and labels were removed; also, all forms of concentrated foods, writing materials and books were confiscated. Many packages were damaged en route and some showed evidence of having been rifled. . . . Items which appeared to be missing were chiefly candy, tobacco and coffee. . . . The Japanese were very sensitive on the subject of these missing articles and threatened to withhold issue of any more packages if they heard any more complaints."[12] (This warning despite the fact that Japanese soldiers were observed smoking American cigarettes.)

Pvt. Leon Elliott recorded in his secret diary his share of the carefully parceled out mail and packages:

> January 6, 1944: First mail arrived from the exchange ship *Gripsholm*.
> January 7, 1944: First Red Cross packages were put out to-day.
> January 8, 1944: Mail from New York & Texas.
> January 26, 1944: I received two letters, one from Pat. H. the other from Mother.
> February 9, 1944: Package from Dad.[13]

At the end of May 1944 a second shipment of Red Cross boxes arrived at Mukden, but the Red Cross double-cross by the Japanese continued, as these boxes were handled in a clandestine way by the Japanese staff. Thompson described the scene this way:

> On the 31st [of May], high excitement prevailed in camp when some workers saw about 400 new boxes marked with the Red Cross delivered into camp on the Japanese side and placed in the Japanese soldiers' quarters. On 1 June, more boxes continued to arrive, but the Japanese were very secretive about them. They attempted to prevent prisoners from learning any information about these boxes and when an interpreter was asked about them he declared that they were for Japanese personnel, saying that "We also receive things from the Red Cross." On the 3rd, the prisoners were given considerable athletic equipment, including baseballs, bats and gloves, soccer and footballs, softballs, etc. Among these were recognized some used baseball mits [sic] that had been "generously" loaned the prisoners on previous occasions by Japanese soldiers and civilians who had claimed the mits as their own personal property.

For over a month, the Japanese had been making free use of these relief goods sent to the prisoners by the International YMCA from the Tokyo branch. It was announced that musical instruments would follow. Major Hankins was informed that there were 2,600 individual Red Cross food packages in camp for the prisoners of war and that this food would be put out in the kitchen rather than to individuals.[14]

Once again, Private Elliott noted in his diary how the Red Cross items were distributed among the prisoners over the next several weeks:

June 20, 1944:	one small bar of Swan soap.
June 21:	one half box of prunes, 8 oz.
June 22:	40 loose cigarettes.
June 26:	small can pork loaf, 3 1/2 oz.
June 28:	1/2 bar chocolate 2 oz.
July 2:	can of pate 6 oz.
July 3:	1/2 can of corned beef 6 oz.
July 4:	1/2 can salmon 3 7/8 oz.
July 5:	40 cigarettes
July 7:	1/2 can butter 1 7/8 oz.
July 8:	can of Welch's grape jam 6 oz.
July 10:	6 oz. of Spam
July 11:	can of butter 3 3/4 oz.[15]

Elliott's listing of tiny portions of food and occasional cigarette supplies indicates that the few Red Cross parcels allowed to be distributed by Colonel Matsuda were portioned out by the POW officers, a procedure described in some detail by WO1 Arnold Bocksel: "The officers discussed what to do and decided the fairest way was to parcel out the contents of the Red Cross boxes and give something to each prisoner from the supply which was released to us."[16]

Over the next few months the ICRC apparently followed up on the distribution of Red Cross supplies, because on August 18, 1944, Lieutenant Murata, the Japanese camp censor, asked a few American officers to write a note stating that the distribution of the Red Cross packages was progressing satisfactorily. In his narrative Thompson said that, actually, the distribution of the food parcels was not unsatisfactory but clothing and medical supplies were being held by the Japanese and the Japanese doctor had announced his intention to take personal responsibility for distribution of medical supplies. Judging by his previous handling of the Japanese medical supplies, prisoners feared that this set-up would be very far from satisfactory; therefore the prisoners in writing these notes were careful to mention only that the distribution of Red Cross food packages was satisfactory (apparently hoping that the ICRC in Geneva would take note of the subtlety). The Japanese failed to note this designation and were quite pleased with the notes, which they said would be forwarded to Red Cross headquarters."[17]

Major Peaty was more explicit in his secret diary, which, unlike Thompson's narrative, was written during captivity: "I hope that medicines and clothing (which we know arrived with the parcels) will not be held up much longer. . . . The Japanese wanted a receipt for the Red Cross medicines, but as they have not been handed over, a hot argument ensued. Eventually a receipt was given for them 'arrived in camp.'"[18]

Some prisoners at the Mukden camp believed that their location was being displayed by the Japanese as a "model camp"; indeed, Japanese propaganda film crews visited for a second time on August 27, 1944. Thompson noted that they gave out candy and tobacco to POWs who participated in the staged musical program. He mentioned that "one of these propaganda men, a Japanese born and raised in America, gave a news broadcast of the sports and movie world, the first news of any kind from the outside that the Japanese had allowed for some time." Thompson recorded that "on 10 September, more than 1,000 letters, mainly from New York and other eastern states, were distributed in camp. One officer received seventy-three letters, some of them containing photographs; however, most of those receiving mail were not so lucky, many receiving two or three letters." But according to Thompson, "the 11th was a sad day for the camp as it was the day of the last issue of the Red Cross food items."[19]

Propaganda teams usually arrived in anticipation of an official inspection, when the camp appearance was being altered. It is possible that the POWs' perception that Mukden was on display was correct, which could account for the unusual fact that Japanese authorities allowed ICRC delegates to visit Mukden on three occasions—three more than Red Cross representatives were allowed in their repeatedly rebuffed attempts to visit POWs and civilians held by the Japanese in other Asian locations.

The second visit to the Mukden POW camp by an ICRC delegate occurred on December 6, 1944, just one day before the disastrous B-29 bomber raid in which nineteen helpless Americans were killed and thirty-five more wounded. But the ICRC delegate, a Mr. Angst, became ill after visiting Mukden and did not file his report in Geneva until the following March. He noted 1,017 American POWs there, with a camp total of 1,117 (the figures and names were supplied by Japanese officials). Other information, again supplied by the Japanese through an interpreter, included dimensions of the camp and living quarters; the food portions allegedly served (noting eggs only on important holidays); and the assertions food was not withheld as a punishment (not true, according to many prisoners who spent time in jail cells there), medical equipment equaled that found in Japanese army hospitals, pay was being distributed (it was not, at least to enlisted men; it was apparently put aside at the camp and discovered after the war), and money could be sent to the POWs' next of kin (no instances were known to have occurred). Disciplinary measures, as reported by Japanese, were noted. Japanese officers claimed discipline was given in English (also not true). The Japanese commandant reported "increased health improved due [to] sincere efforts [of] Kwantung Army Medical Corps" (Unit 731 medical teams, which visited, conducted "tests," and recommended medications that were never delivered). Matsuda even reported to the ICRC representative that he was contemplating purchasing horses and cows for POW recreation.

Delegate Angst also reported on his interview with Major Hankins, noting that it was conducted in the presence of the camp commandant Matsuda:

> Red Cross relief [supplies] greatly appreciated. Food, clothing most welcome. No urgent need for medical, surgical supplies; however should like receiving certain drugs which currently not stocked but possibly required in future (our delegate asked commander for submission [of] relevant list). Red Cross clothing sufficient for only 500 men; among wearing apparel shoes most important. Received large amount [of] mail from America dated September 1943. Very anxious for radiograms, letters. [Major Hankins reported] Colonel Matsuda very fair; excellent man for position; fortunate in having him as commandant. [Hankins was afraid of Matsuda and didn't dare address him personally with any complaints, according to his own testimony at Matsuda's trial postwar.]
>
> Major Robert Peaty, British, very glad of Red Cross surgical supplies. received mail but so far none addressed to Mukden camp. Deplores absence [of] private parcels [and] British Red Cross relief. . . . No permanent dental treatment at camp. Some POW with deteriorating eyesight needing glasses.[20]

Peaty noted Angst's visit in his diary:

> A few panes of glass were given out, to replace some of the cardboard, and meat was issued for the first time since November 23rd. Both, no doubt, were "window-dressing" for the benefit of the Red Cross representative, Mr. Achst [sic], with whom Major Hankins and I had an interview in the same circumstances as before [in the presence of Japanese staff]. He asked many questions and I answered less guardedly than last year, as there are so many things needed that a chance had to be taken about reprisals. As regards treatment, I said that it had greatly improved during the past year, as there had not been nearly so many cases of men being beaten up since Lt. Miki left. I am sure that he got the point—that beatings up are still going on, and at the same time, the Japs thought I was paying them a compliment by saying it had improved. Still, this is the way one had to tackle these people. I also asked for dental treatment if possible, and told him that we had received neither dental nor optical treatment since our arrival. Hankins asked for food and boots, and I asked also for any surgical equipment that could be spared.[21]

One novelty in Angst's visit was that American POWs MSgt. C. J. King and Pfc. Robert Brown were not only present at the meeting with Angst but also allowed to speak to Angst. King "deplores absence of letters from his father" and Brown was "without mail but received [one] private parcel." In a 2005 interview Brown recalled that when he reported receiving no mail from home, Angst wrote a two-page letter to Brown's parents, telling them that Robert was all right. It was the first word his family had received that their son was alive and where he was. He said that in April 1945 he got permission from Oki to send a ten-word telegram to his parents, via the Red Cross, and got a response from them in May 1945. It was the first word from home that he had received.[22] Angst ended his report by noting, "Camp expertly laid out, adequately equipped, competently run." How looks and guarded remarks can deceive.

The third and final visit by an ICRC official to Mukden came in the closing days of the war, on August 5, 1945. Dr. Marcel Junod had been appointed December 1, 1944, to be chief delegate to Tokyo, following the death of Angst the previous June. However, it took eight months for Junod to reach his new post, because the Japanese government would not allow him to fly across "enemy territory" (the United States) from Geneva to reach Tokyo; he literally had to enter Japan by the back door, through Eastern Europe, the Soviet Union, and Manchuria—by rail.

Ironically, while Junod was traveling toward Manchuria, a huge shipment of POW relief supplies left Vladivostok on July 14, 1945, bound for Otper, the terminal of the Trans-Siberian Railway. The hope of the ICRC was that this shipment would establish a practical, new route, which, "if successful . . . may be possible to send large quantities [of supplies] for use of POW in Manchuria." But the logistics were formidable: the railroad tracks that had connected Otper with the Manchurian Railway had been removed, "due probably to border tension," the report observed, so the materials would have to be hauled overland, with the availability of vehicles uncertain. The report concluded: "The Russian government has expressed its willingness to approve such a project providing the Japanese are able to handle the supplies south of the border. This route is worth a trial since the problem of getting supplies to the POW has become extremely difficult."[23] That conclusion is one of the understatements of the century. Although this shipment never reached the prisoners of Mukden, the international community never stopped trying.

When he learned that his route to Japan would take him through Manchuria, Junod insisted on visiting the POW camp at Mukden and on finding and visiting the hero of Corregidor, Gen. Jonathan Wainwright, who had been moved from Formosa in mid-1945 to an as-yet-undisclosed location in Manchuria not far from Mukden. But unlike the visits in November 1943 and December 1944 by Junod's ICRC predecessors, his arrival in Mukden was not prearranged by permission from Tokyo. Junod simply showed up—and no doubt considerably flummoxed Colonel Matsuda, a fact that is evident in the way the Mukden POW commandant handled his unexpected guest.

Junod and his wife, Margherita, arrived at the Mukden POW camp on August 5, 1945, just one day before the first atomic bomb was dropped on Hiroshima.

In his memoir, *Warrior Without Weapons*, Junod expressed considerable frustration at Matsuda's seemingly endless speechifying and his thwarting of Junod's attempts at getting direct answers to his many questions. Recalling his arrival at Mukden, Junod wrote:

> Matsuda was a short man with broad shoulders. He had a big jaw and large teeth, and above a turned-up nose wore large horn-rimmed glasses. Accompanied by two officers, each of whom carried a sheathed saber as he did, he advanced solemnly up the hall of the Hotel Yamato. The three Japanese bowed profoundly three times as they approached, thereby erecting at once that barrier of rigid politeness which distanced them so effectively.
>
> We were driven out to the camp. As we emerged from the suburbs, we came to a large white-wall, barbed wire and a watchtower. The Colonel took us into the officers' mess, where he sank down in an armchair, invited all present to do the same, and made himself comfortable, both hands on the hilt of his saber. About a score of Japanese officers who were present imitated his gestures exactly. After Margherita and I took our places in two chairs, Matsuda proceeded to deliver a lecture as though he were a professor talking to students.
>
> "When the prisoners arrived from the tropics," he recalled in a tone suggesting he was much moved, "they were pitiful. Dressed only in shirts and shorts, they had not stood the icy Manchuria winter very well. Many died of pneumonia and malaria, despite the excellent attention showered on them."
>
> At the end of each sentence, he raised his right hand and tapped himself on the neck two or three times, accompanying the strange gesture with the sonorous exclamation, "Na!" And all his admiring officers responded with an obedient chorus of "Na!"
>
> Margherita and I looked at each other. The time limit for our visit was two hours. Finally I interrupted the Colonel's flow.
>
> "I am impatient to be shown a camp so well organized and so comfortable," I said.
>
> Matsuda found it impossible to do any more stalling, and so with a great clanking of sabers the party rose and paraded outside.[24]

Matsuda's report to Tokyo was even more revealing of his discomfort at Junod's unexpected arrival.

Nevertheless, one thing Junod did insist upon, as a medical doctor, was to visit the POW hospital. It was the first time in the three and a half years of the POWs' captivity that a Red Cross representative had been allowed to do so. His description of this brief encounter, as described earlier, is scathing.

While Junod was making his unprecedented tour of the hospital, Major Peaty noted in his secret diary entry for that day, "A Red Cross representative visited the camp today, but [in contrast to the previous two ICRC visits] no one was allowed any contact with him. I believe his name was Marcel Journeaux [Junod]." The next day, August 6, Peaty's diary entry reads: "All men sent to the factory, presumably to keep them away from the Red Cross visitor."[25] That same day,

Sketch of Dr. Marcel Junod meeting with Gen. Jonathan Wainwright, 1945. From Junod, *Warrior Without Weapons*, artist unknown.

after much persistence on his part, Dr. Junod was taken by Matsuda to Seihan, where the "important prisoners" were being held. Junod had insisted upon being allowed to speak to Gen. Jonathan Wainwright:

> I had difficulty in realizing that I was about to come face to face with the hero of Corregidor, the defender of Singapore [General Percival], the Governor-General of the Dutch East Indies [Starkenborgh] and twelve other soldiers of high rank whose armies were still fighting everywhere in the Pacific. And suddenly a disturbing sight presented itself.
> There they stood upright and motionless in the middle of the room. I should not have been able to distinguish their faces even if I had not involuntarily turned my head away because they bowed low, their arms close to their bodies, as soon as the sabre of Matusda tapped on the floor. The last man in the row refused to submit to the humiliation and remained upright.
> "General Wainwright." My emotion was so great that I could hardly utter the words I had to speak. He maintained an icy reserve towards the Japanese around me. Nothing, it seemed, had broken his spirit. His voice was still vibrant as he replied to the pitiful and absurdly abrupt questions which were all I was allowed to ask him:
> "Have you any request to make?"
> "Certainly. Can I make it now?"
> "No," put in Matsuda at once. "It will have to be made in writing to Tokyo."
> The ghost of a skeptical smile passed over General Wainwright's lips.[26]

The date of this brief interview was August 6, 1945, as the atom bomb fell on Hiroshima. Three weeks later, General Wainwright, in full uniform, greeted Junod in Tokyo with these words: "Now we can talk in peace." But Junod's visit to Mukden haunted him. Six years later, in writing his memoir, he said, "I can still see the camp at Mukden with the bowed backs of its slaves." Partly for this reason, Junod wanted very much to return to the Mukden camp in late August 1945 to oversee its liberation and the repatriation of those POWs whose demeanor haunted him so much. However, a summary of U.S. State Department instructions made it very clear who was to be in charge: the U.S. Military. As they awaited liberation and repatriation, the POWs at Mukden discovered, as did their fellow newly freed prisoners at hundreds of other Japanese camp locations, more than three hundred undistributed Red Cross boxes locked up in the camp commandant's headquarters.

Until the day World War II ended, the Japanese government and its military personnel perpetuated their Red Cross double-cross upon frustrated Red Cross officials, Allied governments, and the suffering prisoners the Allies tried so hard to help.

10

Another Escape
An Ongoing Mystery

William Joseph Lynch was born on March 24, 1919, in Dorchester, Massachusetts, the son of Marie and Daniel Lynch. In 1937, when he was eighteen, he did what many young men did in the Depression years: he enlisted in military service. Billy Lynch chose the Marine Corps. He advanced to the rank of staff sergeant and was assigned to the Service Company of the Fourth Marines Regiment in Shanghai, China. On November 27, 1941, his unit was sent on board the USS *Harrison* to Subic Bay in the Philippines. On December 26 they moved to Corregidor to set up beach defenses following the Japanese attack on Pearl Harbor and the subsequent advances of Japanese forces.[1] When Corregidor fell to the Japanese on May 6, 1942, Staff Sergeant Lynch's unit was confined first to the 92nd Garage on Corregidor, then to Bilibid prison in Manila, and finally to Cabanatuan, where they were placed in the newly created Camp 3. By comparison, the soldiers, sailors, and Marines who had held out on Corregidor were in much better shape than the sick, emaciated survivors of the sixty-five-mile Bataan Death March, and the Corregidor naval officers convinced the Japanese that their men should be separated from the earlier arrivals at Cabanatuan.

Staff Sergeant Lynch, along with other prisoners selected for their special technical skills, was almost relieved to be told that he would be leaving for a "factory work site" in October 1942. He was among the first group of prisoners to leave Cabanatuan. Along with 1,150 other POWs, Lynch was shoved into the holds of Mitsubishi's cargo ship *Tottori Maru* for the thirty-day trip to Pusan, Korea, and on to Mukden, where he was assigned the POW number 607.

Pfc. Roy Weaver, also a member of the Fourth Marines on Corregidor, was assigned POW number 610, and since the prisoners were sent by number to the nineteen barracks in the first camp, Weaver wound up in a bunk near Lynch. "Numbers 608 and 609 died that first winter," Weaver recalled, "So Lynch and I spread out a little and had a bit more space between us. I remember he kept saying, 'I can't handle this' many times. He made a lot of remarks about escaping.

Once we moved to the new camp [in late July 1943], we were not in the same barracks and I didn't see him again."[2]

On May 2, 1944, the Japanese camp staff sent about one hundred POWs, including Lynch, to the Manchu Leather factory, which was much closer to Mukden City than the main camp. A subcamp was set up near the factory to house the POW workers. At the leather factory the POWs made belts and gun holsters for the Imperial Japanese Army, sometimes decorating the leather with uncomplimentary graffiti, according to Pfc. Herschel Bouchey of the Army. The working conditions at Manchu Leather were toxic; several POWs assigned there recalled that a significant number of them developed respiratory problems and tuberculosis. After a couple of weeks at this new work site, one restless Marine had had enough.

Lynch realized that this new subcamp was fairly close to Mukden City and less well fortified than the main camp. Perhaps he hoped that the limited amount of Chinese he had picked up while stationed in Shanghai might help him find some friendly Chinese in Mukden. On May 18, 1944, a warm spring night, Lynch walked out of Sub-camp 2 and headed for the city.

Sometime during the night he was spotted by a military policeman in Masenjiazi, a village near Mukden (now part of Shenyang). He was ordered to stop but began to run away and was shot in the leg. He was beaten and later transported back to the main camp on a stretcher. Weaver remembered being in the yard at that time, and he could see that the man on the stretcher was Lynch. "He was carried into the first building inside the camp—it was an anteroom we passed through on our way to work. I didn't see him go out; he was gone when I came back, and we never saw him again."[3]

As had been true a year earlier when three prisoners escaped, punishment was swift and encompassing for the men at Sub-camp 2. Lt. William Thompson described the event and follow-up to it:

> On the night of 18 May [1944], there was some unusual activity on the part of the Japanese, consisting of much bustling around and the setting up of a machine gun in front of one of the barracks. The prisoners thought this was part of an air raid drill, but the next day they learned that eight men from the branch camp were put in the guard house. Rumor had it that one had tried to escape and was wounded in the leg at the time of capture. This later turned out to be true and the man who had escaped was sent to a military prison. This man, a U.S. Marine sergeant, was never returned to the Mukden Prisoner of War Camp, but he was carried on the roll there, and at TENKO [daily roll call] the section leader of his former section always had to report, "Ichi mei, cho-ikki". This meant, "One Man in Military Prison" according to the Japanese. . . . As a result of the attempted escape from the branch camp, several men were in the guard house as punishment for not immediately reporting the escape or for being in some other way implicated. Thirty-two men from that camp,

these men being among what the Japanese considered as bad actors, were exchanged with men from the main camp. It was more difficult to escape from the main camp.[4]

The eight men who were on rotating night "fire watch" duty were confined to the guard house, accused of in some way helping Lynch or "looking the other way" as he made his escape.

Despite the fact that Lynch had been reported "in military prison" every day at roll call since May 19, 1944, when Lt. Col. James F. Donovan of the OSS arrived at the camp on August 29, 1945, to supervise the orderly evacuation and repatriation of all prisoners, he was initially told that Lynch was present in the camp. When he learned that Lynch had been in a military prison elsewhere for the past fifteen months, Donovan sent the following cable message to headquarters in Hsian: "S/SGT William J. Lynch 256599 USMC originally reported as member of this POW camp before processing team arrived is not actually present. Was caught trying to escape in May 1944 and staff of POW camp believed he was in a prison in Mukden. All efforts to locate him have failed so far. He may be in dungeon in Port Arthur and we will try to find him there."[5]

After Donovan's search of all prisons in Mukden City failed to yield any information about Staff Sergeant Lynch, he questioned the Japanese camp staff more intensely. When they speculated that perhaps Lynch had been taken to a *Kempeitai* (Japanese military police) prison in Port Arthur, Donovan set out by plane to Dairen in the company of a Russian officer. He hoped to continue on to Port Arthur. He later described what happened to that effort:

> As the two Russian planes in which Lt. Kalmanoff and I had flown to Dairen were being serviced all day of the 13th [of September 1945] I decided to try to go to Port Arthur myself in a Navy Jeep to make one last attempt to find Sgt. Lynch or any trace of him. I made the error of asking the Russian commandant of the city of Dairen for permission to go to Port Arthur. Permission was emphatically refused and I was told that if I tried it I would probably be shot by patrols. I was convinced that further argument was useless and gave up after again requesting that the Russians keep searching for Lynch as they claimed to have been doing for sometime.[6]

Five months earlier, on April 14, 1945, Marie Lynch sent a letter to her son: "Dear Bill, How are you. We are all fine. Eleanor [his older sister] is back home. Uncle George is very sick. Why don't you write. Write soon. Love from all, Ma."[7] Her letter was returned to her, undelivered, with no explanation. Little did she know her son was probably already dead by April 1945.

Colonel Donovan departed the Mukden POW camp on September 19, 1945. He concluded his report on the evacuation of the camp with this observation: "I believe that everything was completely settled and nothing left to be done unless

Sgt. Lynch and Pvt. [Berry] Howard [who had gone AWOL after being denied permission to marry a Russian girl] eventually show up."[8]

After the colonel filed his report with headquarters, the Marine Corps officially declared SSgt. William Lynch dead in October 1945. Marie Lynch was notified by mail, but the Marine Corps could not tell her what had happened to her son or why and where he had died. And there were no remains to send home, no chance for a proper funeral. But Dorchester did not forget the Marine who never came back from the war. In the 1950s there was a ceremony at the intersection near his home, which was renamed William J. Lynch Square. Still, Marie Lynch went to her grave never getting any answers to why her son remained unaccounted for.

Pvt. William J. Lynch, USMC, 1937. Lynch family photo.

And there the mystery of Lynch remained for the next sixty-three years, until 2008, when Shenyang University professor Jing Yang decided to travel to Port Arthur (now Lushun) in hopes of finding someone who could tell him more about what happened at the *Kempeitai* prison in 1944–45. Yang, who in 2005 had successfully located a witness to the recapture of the three 1943 escapees from the Mukden camp, was once again successful. This time he found three men in Lushun who spent time at the *Kempeitai* prison, either as workers or as inmates. All three remembered just one American prisoner who had been brought there in 1944. Yang questioned them closely. Were they sure this Caucasian was not British, or Australian, or even Russian? No, they all insisted, he was definitely American. (Perhaps they had heard him speak, with his unmistakably American, New England accent.) And they told Yang more. The American had been tortured and finally executed. His remains, they believed, had been buried in a one-acre field near the prison, where the remains of deceased prisoners were known to have been interred. So Lynch was probably dead before the end of 1944.

Yang's findings about the possible location of Lynch's remains attracted the attention of a privately funded organization, Moore's Marauders, headquartered in Scottsdale, Arizona, which has as its mission locating and retrieving the remains of military personnel missing from all wars. While his organization began raising funds to send a team of radar, forensic, and archaeological experts to Lushun to search the field Yang had identified, CEO Ken Moore enlisted the aid of Marie Daly, library director at the New England Historic Genealogical Society in Boston. Daly searched Boston City records and found Lynch's sister Eleanor's date of birth and a 1947 telephone directory listing showing Eleanor and her husband Harold Hinesley living at the Lynch family home at 57 Victory Road, Dorchester. Through Social Security records Daly discovered that Eleanor had subsequently moved to Brockton, Massachusetts. Using motor vehicle records, she then discovered that Eleanor's daughter Janet had applied for a driver's license from the Brockton address. A search of vital records of the state gave Daly the name of Janet's twin sister, Judith. Using the Ancestry database maintained by the genealogical society, Daly obtained addresses and telephone numbers for the twins and subsequently located their brother, Chris, and younger sister Susan. The twins and Chris have agreed to provide DNA samples to Moore's Marauders.

In October 2009 Moore's Marauders members Ryan Bach and Mark Voner, financed by the organization, visited Shenyang and Lushun, China. They met with Professor Jing Yang of Shenyang University, local government officials, and members of the American consulate staff. The team signed a "Memorandum of Understanding" with local university and government officials, toured the partially restored Mukden POW camp site and museum, and traveled to Dailan (Dairen) and the Lushun (formerly Port Arthur) prison site, where they met with officials at the museum that has been created at the former *Kempeitai* prison. The team received the full support of museum, university, and local officials in both locations, as well as staff at the American consulate in Shenyang. A team of scientific, archaeological, and forensic anthropological experts is scheduled, beginning in April 2010, to return to Lushun to search for the remains of SSgt. William Lynch.

The hope is that the field in Lushun will yield some bones containing DNA that matches that of Eleanor's children. If that happens, Staff Sergeant Lynch can finally be brought home to Dorchester. So the final chapter of this Marine's story is still to be written, as this book goes to press.

11

B-29s Bring Death, Hope, and Rescue

On December 1, 1944, an earthquake shook the ground in the Mukden area. A Native American soldier remarked to Australian doctor Capt. Des Brennan that the earthquake was a portent of disaster. He was right. On December 7, 1944, the third anniversary of Japan's attack on Pearl Harbor, the United States Air China Command marked the occasion by sending a sortie of eighty-three B-29 Bombers to raid the industrial complex of Mukden. The pilots were aware, from previous intelligence and Red Cross reports, that there was a large POW camp nearby, but they had no way of knowing that the camp was just one kilometer from a prime target, a munitions factory in Mukden City. In violation of the Geneva Conventions, the Japanese consistently failed to mark POW camp sites, including Mukden, as well as ships transporting prisoners.

During the summer of 1944, the prisoners at Mukden participated in a few air-raid drills. A siren would sound, and, said Pvt. William "Dingle" Bell, "we had to run to the search shed, then after searching we were counted, then had to run back to the camp [from the MKK factory], and lay on the parade ground until given the 'All Clear.'"[1] Despite repeated requests by American and British officers, the Japanese camp staff refused to allow the prisoners to dig air-raid shelters (trenches) anywhere in the camp. But on December 7, 1944, as Bell recalled,

> something seemed different. The guards weren't laughing as much as they had during the other runs back to camp. They were shouting "Speedo!" all the time to urge us to hurry. We got back to the barracks and got any extra clothes needed, then out onto the parade ground. After a short while we saw the vapor trails then heard the engines of the bombers overhead. There were smaller trails around them as Jap fighters had a go at them. We heard bombs falling, saw a great gush of flame as a bomber exploded from collision with a fighter. Then pieces fell from it, turning over and over in the air. All of the time sounds of bombs falling some distance away from us. Another bomber mortally wounded falling while laying fleecy looking eggs which turned out to be

its crew parachuting to the ground, the smoke pouring out of smudge pots to protect the factory and the camp, the smoke pouring out of the city from bomb damage or more smudge pots, who knows? The delighted Americans saluting the waves of American bombers flying over, the change to horror when one plane left the formation and "shook" itself to loosen two stick bombs and two silver eggs of doom streaking like lightning flashes towards twelve hundred men strewn all over the parade ground, each one thinking: "This is it."

I heard the scream building up to a crescendo as the bomb fell madly towards me and following the rules I took a deep breath then started letting the air out slowly and closed my eyes. There was an ear-splitting explosion and all the rest of the breath was forced out of me. I slowly opened my eyes. It was dark. I closed my eyes again, waited for a few minutes and tried again. It was light again. I looked around and saw chaos. Piles of clothing all over the place, even a pair of trousers draped over the barbed wire nearby but with shoes hanging from the cuffs, a great hole in the brick fence with a Jap guard looking thru it, then panic as people realized that others had been killed by their sides or at their feet or mortally wounded; men screaming for stretcher bearers at the sight of a dear friend torn to pieces by bomb fragments.

I was still shocked by the explosion and still not comprehending. In front of my face I saw a hat peak and thought: "that looks like an old hat, yet those hats were only issued in June or July." I turned it over. It had brain tissue spread all over it, then it dawned on me, somebody had died in that explosion. I looked around me again. That pile of clothes was a pile of dead bodies. Those trousers were the last half of a body. That coat did not have a head coming out of the top. That man [Pvt. Melvin] "Bumgarner" was saluting; did not have his saluting arm now and he also had a hole in his head and brains from his head were all over [Cpl.] Jim Clancy's coat. Bumgarner survived this duo of injuries; apparently those brains weren't needed. It was the peak of his hat I had found.[2]

Sgt. John Zenda said the impact of the bomb "blew me up in the air, blew off all the buttons on my coat, and shattered my eardrums. I felt myself fading in and out and remember thinking, 'God, please help me.' I was bleeding from the ears as I flew in the air."[3]

Cpl. Joseph Petak chronicled his personal recollections of the raid, beginning with his first sight of the bombers: "There were nine of them [streamers]. . . . They were high, very high. Tiny, tiny gnats. Japanese fighters. The hospital patients that could not walk had been brought out [to the parade ground] by the corpsmen . . . [to lie on the ground]. . . . One of the men close by jumped to his feet and ran around in blind terror. . . . 'Tell them to let us out! We'll all be killed here!' . . . There was all hell spread around the southwest corner of the compound. . . . The Jap interpreters were not found anywhere around. . . . Here for the first time in three years the Americans had struck against the treacherous yellow bastards!"[4]

Major Peaty described the effectiveness of the air raid in his December 7, 1944, diary entry:

A salvo of bombs fell close by, dealing very effectively with a small arms ammunitions factory about 1 km north of the camp. (I believe twelve bombs hit the factory: at any rate, it never functioned again.) A second wave of B-29s came over, and two bombs fell into the camp, one of which hit No. 2 Barracks latrine and set it afire, although it did not explode. The other, which did explode, dropped right among us on the parade ground, causing 54 casualties, 16 being killed outright. There is only one stretcher in camp, but we tore down goalposts, etc. and carried the wounded on overcoat litters into hospital, and got them all there before the next wave came over. . . . Immediately after the raid, and while the Japanese were still out of control, we dug slit trenches all over the parade-ground, in spite of previously having been forbidden to do so. Sgt. Russell of the [medical corps] did excellent work in instructing those acting as stretcher bearers as to which of the casualties should be taken to hospital, and Pvt. Vaughn [also a medic], although stone deaf, and liable to drop at the slightest exertion, from a weak heart, went at once to the hospital and did good work. Discipline was superb.

The next day Peaty wrote about amputations and the three additional deaths, noting, "The Japanese emergency lighting system consisted of five candles for the whole camp, but Dr. Brennan had managed to conceal a packet of candles he brought from Singapore, right up to now, and with the aid of these the doctors operated on the wounded up to 1 A.M. on the night of the bombing, when they had to give up as the candles had all been consumed." Thompson added, "Many volunteers pressed into service as medical corpsmen and doctors worked constantly without rest in trying to save the lives of the wounded."[5]

The death toll would have been much higher had not the entire medical team in the POW hospital performed so heroically. Looking back, members of the POW medical team agreed it was truly a miracle that "only" nineteen prisoners had perished in the December 7 raid. Pfc. Robert Brown described some of those creative heroics as they worked through the night to save the lives of the wounded: "I took a tin can and bent the lid up to be a reflector for candlelight. I lit cotton swabs with alcohol for light."[6] Brown recalled that "Dr. Shabart was on the floor, drunk, after the air raid. The Japanese camp staff beat him trying to find out where he had gotten the alcohol. Dr. Oki had let the American doctors back in the hospital in November, but he kicked them out again, after the air raid."[7]

Brown earned a letter of commendation from Colonel Matsuda, which read in part, "Especially for his sincere and strenuous efforts that he carried on through the night for the high attainment of arranging and polishing the surgical instruments and equipment and remaking bandages in accordance with the instructions of Nipponese Medical Staff, I hereby commend and reward him with a prize." (It was a pack of cigarettes.)[8] And at the end of the war, Brown received a letter of commendation from the U.S. War Department, dated April 30, 1946, which read in part, "You helped care for fellow prisoners suffering from . . .

the destruction of an air raid in which 54 prisoners were either killed or seriously injured. Your unselfish efforts on behalf of the ill and wounded were admirable."[9]

As for the crews of the B-29s damaged by Japanese air and ground fire, apparently one crew member survived the midair collision of the first aircraft, and according to Brown, the Japanese chained the wounded aviator to the motor of the downed plane and put him on display in a Mukden City park, where he died, still chained to the motor.[10]

All crew members of the second damaged B-29 parachuted to earth, and fourteen aviators in all were captured by Japanese soldiers. According to an account written by crew member Olen Hermann, the crew spent their first nine days of captivity in a Mukden jail and the next ninety-eight days in solitary confinement, after which they were moved to a compound built for them near the camp but isolated from the other prisoners.

When prisoners working in the POW kitchen at the Mukden camp were told to make up additional pots of meals, they suspected these might be for delivery to the captured B-29 aviators, since many had seen several parachutes floating to earth during the air raid. Capt. Des Brennan recalled hearing that kitchen staff prisoners hollowed out the handles of pots sent out to their unknown destination, in which they placed notes asking about the identity of the recipients. "In this way we found out who they were," he said.[11]

After the camp was liberated, the B-29 crew members came in and confirmed to their newly freed fellow POWs that two bombs had stuck in the bomb bay of one plane and had come loose while the plane was circling the camp, its pilot hoping to shake them loose over their intended target. They apologized profusely for the error and the deaths it had caused, but because the camp was not marked in any way, the aviators had no way of knowing that Allied prisoners were confined just a short distance from their targets.

After the December 7 raid, the Japanese lost no time in exploiting it for propaganda purposes. On December 11 prisoners who wished to do so were invited to draw up wills to be kept in a safe at the camp, and forwarded, when and if needed, to their nation's War Department. On December 12 a secret message was sent to Japan's propaganda office in Budapest and intercepted by Allied intelligence. The message, labeled "Propaganda notice #103," reads, "On the 7th in the Mukden raid by B-29s, the prisoner of war shelter was hit, causing about 4 deaths. In the future please propagandize the fact that such indiscriminant bombing will result in self-destruction of the enemy."[12]

It is worth noting the use of the word "shelter" in this message. Far be it from the Japanese to admit that they provided no air-raid shelter for their prisoners at the "model" Mukden camp, and that they prohibited the POWs from digging any prior to the December 7 raid. Also, the prisoners reported as killed in this message—four—were all killed at the shelter, thereby avoiding mention of the fact that nearly all POW deaths occurred on the parade ground, where prisoners were forced to lie, unprotected, in the open. And no reference is made to the fact that the camp was not marked in any way.

Four days later, on December 16, Thompson described the further attempt at propaganda exploitation within the camp, which met with limited success:

> On 16 December, Lt. Murata [the camp censor] assembled the prisoner officers and told them they must write an objection to the bombing of the prison camp. He also sent an enlisted man interpreter to the hospital to get similar radio messages from the patients, particularly those wounded by the bomb. He said that these objections were to be broadcast by radio to the Allied China Theater headquarters. When these objections were written, many of them told of the lack of air raid shelters for the prisoners and that the Japanese had refused requests by the prisoners to construct trenches and fox holes previous to the time of the bombing. Other letters described the nearness of military objectives. When Lt. Murata read these letters, he became so angry he tore them all up and reassembled the officers, telling them specifically the things they could mention. Some officers declined to write, but those who did tried to put as much information as possible in them with the hope of identifying the location of the camp so that on future raids it would not be hit. These letters appeared to satisfy the Japanese, but they were again angered on reading some of the letters turned in by hospital patients, some of whom had written such things as: "We don't care what happens to us, hit them with all you got."[13]

Despite the terror, loss of life, and psychological impact of being "invited" to draw up wills, the prisoners at Mukden knew their redemption was nearing. Again it came from the sky, eight long months later. During the first few months of 1945, the prisoners at Mukden began wondering just how long it might be before the war ended. Weeks? Months? Surely it would be soon, because U.S. aircraft were obviously dominating the airspace all over Japanese-occupied territory, even Manchuria.

Australian private George Harriss had arranged to pay some of his gambling winnings to a Japanese civilian working at the MKK factory in exchange for copies of Japanese newspapers. Capt. Des Brennan stated in his oral memoir that a New Zealander, a Lieutenant Gregg, could read Japanese. Suddenly the POW grapevine was able to circulate daily updates of American victories throughout the Pacific and the relentless progress toward Japan's home islands. But POW optimism was tinged with apprehension, as some prisoners said they noticed Japanese machine guns placed in the towers around the perimeter of the main camp and pointing inward. This was widely reported at many other POW camps, from Thailand to Formosa to the Philippines and the home islands, especially during July 1945, along with the burning of camp records during the first weeks of August.[14] Finally POW apprehension turned to real fear during the week of August 8, after prisoners learned that Russian troops had invaded Manchuria and were rapidly heading toward Mukden. What might happen to them in Russian custody?

Meanwhile American military commanders had several reasons to worry about the fate of our prisoners of war. First, on August 1, 1944, British intelligence had intercepted a message from the Japanese vice commander of war circulated to the commandants of all POW camps in the Japanese Empire. The message clarified under what circumstances a camp commandant could take matters into his own hands without waiting for orders from Tokyo to place in motion the longstanding directive to execute all prisoners if enemy invasion seemed imminent. The August 1944 message said if a commandant thought he might be surrendering his position, or if he saw signs that prisoners might be planning a breakout, he could commence executions. The message went on to make suggestions of methods for execution—mass bombing, poisonous smoke, poisons, drowning, decapitation—and ended with the chilling sentence: "In any case, it is the aim not to allow the escape of a single one, to annihilate them all, and not to leave any traces."[15] This directive had already been carried out on Wake Island in October 1943 and on Palawan Island in December 1944; in both cases the POW camp commanders thought U.S. invasion was imminent. It didn't happen either place until the war ended. But the POW executions did happen in those locations, and our military commanders knew it.

Second, on February 9, 1945, our War Department Military Intelligence Service circulated a memorandum on possible biological warfare use by the Japanese, citing an intercepted Japanese army directive sent August 13, 1943, outlining methods for inoculating Japanese troops against contagious diseases. The formulas were to be prescribed by the chief of the Bureau of Medicine, noting that products of the Kwantung Army Water Purification Unit (Unit 731) "may be used in Forces stationed in Manchuria." The U.S. intelligence memorandum comments that "[Japanese] PWs have also stated that Water Purification Units are propagating bacteria for BW [biological warfare] purposes."[16]

Some historians believe that the Russians invaded Manchuria to give themselves a place at the bargaining table when the victorious Allied powers divided the territories of the Japanese Empire. But the fact is that at the February 1945 Yalta Conference, Soviet premier Josef Stalin secretly promised President Roosevelt and Prime Minister Churchill that three months after the Germans surrendered to Allied forces, the Soviets would open up an eastern war front for the Japanese by invading Manchuria.[17] So when Germany surrendered on May 8, 1945, Premier Stalin, true to his word, ordered Soviet forces to invade Manchuria on August 8, 1945, exactly three months after the war ended in Europe. The fact that August 8 fell between the August 6 and August 9 atomic bombings of Hiroshima and Nagasaki was coincidental. However, the terms of the Yalta agreement remained secret until 1947, fueling speculation as to Soviet motives.

When Soviet tanks and troops began rolling toward Harbin and Mukden, Gen. Albert Wedemeyer, headquarters commander of the China theater, ordered Col. Richard Heppner, commander of the OSS, China theater, to prepare a small OSS team to secure the POW camp at Mukden by American forces and to locate and rescue Gen. Jonathan Wainwright and other top Allied officers who had been sent with him from Formosa to the vicinity of Mukden in December 1944.

The operation was code-named Cardinal Mission. The team was headed by Maj. James T. Hennessy and included Maj. Robert Lamar (a medical doctor); Sgt. Edward A. Starz; Sgt. Fumio Kido, a nisei born in Hawaii to Japanese parents; Cheng Shih-wu, a Nationalist Chinese officer, and Cpl. (later SSgt.) Hal Leith, who was selected because he was fluent in both Chinese and Russian.

On August 16, 1945, the day after Emperor Hirohito announced on the radio that he had accepted the Allied terms for surrender, the Cardinal Mission team parachuted into a field about two miles from the Mukden POW camp. Leaving the other two to guard their supplies, four of them, including Corporal Leith, began walking toward the camp but were intercepted by a Japanese patrol. When Leith told them Japan had surrendered the previous day, they didn't believe him, not yet having heard the news. Major Lamar went back to the landing site under Japanese guard; all three team members were stripped and beaten. The other three were taken into an empty building then blindfolded and led to a vehicle that took all six to *Kempeitai* headquarters in Mukden City. Fortunately, the *Kempeitai* colonel had heard of the surrender on the radio, although he did not yet have instructions from Tokyo. However, he did tell the team that they were his "guests" and not prisoners of war. He said he would contact Tokyo that evening; meanwhile, the team would be taken to the Mukden POW camp. After a long wait they were taken to the camp. But the *Kempeitai* colonel warned that Colonel Matsuda also had no instructions from Tokyo and probably wouldn't let the team meet with any POWs. Indeed, that is what Matsuda said when he met the team at the camp entrance. He said they could stay at the Yamato Hotel in Mukden, but before the team left the camp site, Leith signaled "OK" with his hands and waved to the POWs watching from windows.

The next morning, August 17, the OSS team was taken from the hotel to the *Kempeitai* headquarters, where the colonel bowed deeply, said he was surrendering to them, and offered to commit hara-kiri in front of them. They told him to stay and keep order with Japanese troops in Mukden. As they were getting back in the truck, the formerly surly Japanese soldier who had sternly told them "No talk!" the day before, walked up to Leith and said, "Hey! I have a brother in L.A. I wonder if you know him?"

This time Matsuda invited the team into his office and sent for the American POW commander, Maj. Gen. George Parker, who bowed as he entered, before he saw the team. They informed him, "No more bowing—the war is over, and we have come to get all the POWs back home." Leith ran out into the yard— the first free American the prisoners had seen in three years and four months. Looking huge at 172 pounds next to the emaciated POWs, Leith told them the news and then was peppered with questions:

> How did the 1943 and '44 Rose Bowl games end?
> Who won the last three World Series?
> Is Shirley Temple dead? [A favorite Japanese propaganda line.]
> Is Roosevelt really dead? What did he die of?
> Who is president?
> When did the war actually end?
> Who is prime minister of England?
> Is Queen Wilhelmina of the Netherlands still alive?
> How much pay do Army Ranks get now?

Leith said in his memoir, "It was one of the happiest days of my life, even though all of the POWs looked so bad."[18] Then he set out for Hsian, accompanied by Major Lamar, to rescue General Wainwright.

Liberated B-29 crew, 1945. *Back row:* SSgt. Olen Hermann, MSgt. Daniel Stieber, Capt. John Campbell, Capt. Benjamin Lipscomb, Capt. George Matsko, Capt. Richard McCormick, SSgt. Arnold Pope, Capt. Virgil Unruh. *Front row:* Sgt. George Brown, SSgt. Kenneth Beckwith, SSgt. Ralph Davidson, Sgt. Aaron Eldred, Sgt. Elbert Edwards, Sgt. Walter Huss. Tenth Air Force photo.

August 16–17, 1945, were the happiest days for a lot of others at Mukden, namely, the prisoners themselves. MM John Guidos of the Navy probably reflected the mood of many when he stated,

> Things progressed, always looking brighter, until the 16th of August when the six men parachuted on the Japanese airfield, risking their lives to do it. They were brought into camp about four hours later. Naturally it didn't take long for the word to get around of their mission among such an inquisitive group as we were. Later on they told us they came for us, but I still think that their premature arrival was timed to prevent any atrocities that the Japs were sure to have in mind and would no doubt have committed. What an elation in the camp that night. It was like being born again.
>
> Next morning we were notified by Maj. Gen. Parker that there was an armistice in effect. We were asked to behave ourselves and act like Americans. On the 20th a Russian captain came into camp and with the usual Russian flourish and showmanship told us that we were free in the name of the Red Army, etc.
>
> That evening the Russians disarmed the Japanese and our own guard was posted. We watched the proceeding with great joy and started to jeer at the Japs. The colonel [Matsuda], commanding officer, was a great one for writing speeches, beginning with "My Dear Boys, Take care of yourselves. My staff and I are working day and night for your welfare . . ." The next day he would reduce our rations. This we were throwing into his face and enjoying it. We were silenced by Gen. Parker and told to act like Americans, and not to make any demonstrations. We just wanted to jeer at them, make them lose face, and be somewhat repaired for the deprivations, insults and beatings we endured under their regime.[19]

Cpl. Joseph Petak and his friends had seen the OSS team's parachutes drop from the B-24 on August 16:

> Men, four white men, Americans, marched around the corner of the brick building. The Americans were dressed in Air Corps coveralls. . . . One was a Jap in an American uniform, and the other was plainly a Chinaman. . . . A blonde young soldier smiled and waved at us. . . . "The parachutists!" I mumbled. . . . A piercing whistle was let out by one of the team. . . . Two of them waved to us. One man clasped his hands and waved them over his head. "The War is Over!" Hell broke loose in Mukden. It was as happy a hell as one could imagine. Men grabbed each other and danced around the compound. Everything broke all of a sudden. . . . There was no way to hold back the emotions that broke loose. There were hundreds of crying men. It was the end! Three years! Three years and four months! The end! THANK GOD![20]

In his diary entry for August 16, Major Peaty wrote,

> Six men were brought into camp today, and from the fact that they were smoking more than the regulation distance from an ash-tray, we knew they were not Prisoners-of-War. After an unusually good supper, all prisoners were released from the guardhouse. (Just after breakfast some men told me that a

large plane had flown very low over the camp, and that six men had bailed out, they thought on to a small airfield nearby, and that the plane had made a circuit, dropped a number of coloured parachutes, and flown off. They were convinced that Russian paratroops had seized the airfield. I pointed out that paratroops were used in the hundreds, not in half-dozens.) However, the six men who were brought into camp that evening were a Col. Donovan [Maj. Peaty confused Maj. Hennessy with OSS Col. Donovan, who did arrive at the camp two weeks later] and three other officers and an American-born Chinese, and an American-born Japanese, both interpreters. On landing they were seized, beaten up, and nearly executed before they could induce the Japanese to look at their credentials, as the Japanese military knew nothing of the capitulation. They did succeed just in time, and were brought to camp.

The major's August 17 diary entry begins, "The senior Dutch, American and British officers were sent for by the Commandant, and officially informed that an Armistice had been signed between Britain, U.S.A. and the Netherlands on one hand, and Japan on the other, but that it is believed that fighting continues against Russia (who declared war on Japan on the 9th of this month, as we well know.) We presumably wait with what patience we can for arrangements to be made for our return." He also noted that more than thirty thousand pieces of mail addressed to POWs were distributed, some more than three years old.

Lt. William Thompson's narrative correctly identifies the members of the OSS team but adds this detail: "Two days previous to their arrival, there was supposed to have been a plane over the area to drop leaflets in Japanese and English about the mission of the six men. As it turned out, these leaflets had not been dropped and the OSS team had parachuted into hostile unprepared country."[21] Thompson also noted the arrival of the Russians on August 20 at the camp, declaring the prisoners free. And that evening General Parker took command of the camp.

The next evening, August 21, a B-24 circled low over Mukden, dropping the leaflets that were supposed to have been dropped a week earlier. They were signed by Lt. Gen. Albert C. Wedemeyer, commander, Headquarters, U.S. Forces in China:

NOTICE TO ALLIED PRISONERS OF
WAR AND CIVILIAN INTERNEES

The Japanese Government has accepted the Allied peace terms set forth in the Potsdam Declaration. Final negotiations are being concluded.

An official representative is on his way for humanitarian purposes and liaison with this headquarters. He will be an initial, pre–Allied occupation representative in the interests of welfare needs and general conditions in the area or camp to which he is sent.

He will coordinate with the Red Cross and Japanese Military and Government, all plans to secure the security of the personnel concerned, to take emergency action to properly house, feed, clothe and furnish medical assistance to such personnel, and to assist in maintaining order in camps awaiting occupational forces.

He will *not* have authority to act for the Allied Forces in rendering any decisions, military, civil or otherwise. Until such time as Allied occupational forces arrive to accept the surrender of Japanese military forces, those military forces are responsible for all such control and decisions in conformity with the terms of surrender and the dictates of the Supreme Allied Command.[22]

Despite this announcement, and the scenes described by Machinist's Mate Guidos, Corporal Leith, and Corporal Petak showing American POWs clearly receiving the news of their liberation by fellow Americans, it is puzzling that many Mukden survivors continue to say, in postwar statements, interviews, and memoirs, that they were liberated by the Russian army.

Meanwhile, Leith and Lamar succeeded in rescuing General Wainwright and the other American, British, and Dutch high-ranking officers with him at Hsian. It took until August 27, on broken-down trucks, over muddy roads and on foot, and finally on decrepit railroad trains for the party to reach Mukden City. On August 28 Leith saw Wainwright off to Japan by air. Before departing, Wainwright told Leith that in bringing the officers safely from Hsian, he had done the job as well as any major could have done. Hal Leith cherished that remark, and he quoted it often in later years.

As for General Wainwright, he got a hero's welcome from troops, liberated POWs, and the press, everywhere he went. This irked Supreme Commander Gen. Douglas MacArthur, who was aware of the resentment POWs felt toward him. In addition he nursed a grudge against Wainwright, dating back to their days at West Point, when Cadet Wainwright bested Cadet MacArthur in competitions. MacArthur neglected to invite Wainwright to the ceremony for the signing of the Instrument of Surrender on board the USS *Missouri* in Tokyo Bay on September 2, 1945, until the White House ordered him to do so.[23]

For the men of Mukden, it was enough to know that General Wainwright also had been rescued, and was on his way home, as they soon would be. The American OSS team liberated and secured a total of 1,671 prisoners, including 1,318 Americans—their ranks swelled by the influx of high-ranking officers and other prisoners sent to Mukden from Formosa in the spring of 1945 in an attempt to hide them from "the enemy" (the United States) in Manchuria.

12

The Long Road Back

On August 24, 1945, the U.S. ambassador to Moscow, W. Averill Harriman, sent a message to the secretary of state in Washington responding to the State Department's request of August 21 asking him to contact Soviet foreign minister Vyacheslav Molotov regarding the arrival of Soviet troops at the Mukden POW camp on August 19. There was, of course, concern about the American POWs. Ambassador Harriman's message read, "Have transmitted to Molotov Department's message #1883, Aug. 21, regarding American prisoners of war in vicinity of Mukden. In order to expedite return of these men to American control it would seem desirable to make as soon as possible a concrete proposal to Soviet authorities as to procedure by which we would wish Soviet government to turn them over to us." Whether the State Department was aware of the Cardinal Mission's arrival at the POW camp on August 16 is unclear. What is clear is that the State Department, in responding to Harriman's suggestion, replied that same day, August 24, stating clearly that the "repatriation of POWs and civilian internees [was] to be by Military Commanders in Field. IRC [ICRC] to deal directly with Commanders."[1]

The next day, August 25, a follow-up State Department message was even stronger, officially disallowing "U.S. Foreign Service officers to assist in the repatriation of POWs and civilian internees, which is being handled by the Military Authorities." The ICRC's Tokyo representative, Marcel Junod, who had been so moved by the subservience of the Mukden POWs during his August 5 visit to the camp, was very anxious to participate in their repatriation, but the State Department made its position crystal clear. Junod had been firmly instructed to "take no action in the evacuation of POWs" and was informed that the Army was "work[ing] out plans."[2] Also, General Wedemeyer was not about to let the Russians have control of our POWs. As far as he was concerned, the OSS team remained in control of the POW camp, with command having been turned over to General Parker.

On August 26, two days after Ambassador Harriman's "suggestion," General Wedemeyer gave a special order to OSS commander Colonel Heppner to dispatch POW Recovery Team No. 1 to Mukden. The team was headed by the OSS's Col. James F. Donovan, and it arrived on August 29 at Mukden Municipal Airport, where they were met by the OSS's Maj. James T. Hennessy, Maj. Robert Lamar of the Cardinal Mission, and Major Watson of the special OSS Air-Ground Aid Service (AGAS), the chief mission of which was the recovery of POWs.

At the airport the Russian commandant's reception of Colonel Donovan was "not very friendly."[3] The prickly Russian wanted to know why Donovan had brought so many men with him (Recovery Team No. 1 had nineteen members), why they were carrying sidearms, and when they were leaving. The Russians were clearly annoyed that Americans had gotten to the camp ahead of them. Ultimately, General Parker agreed to continue with camp administration, leaving Colonel Donovan free to concentrate on processing and evacuation plans—and to keep an eye on the Russians.

On August 30 fifty-eight former POWs most in need of medical care were evacuated by air to Kunming. Among them was Pvt. Eddy Laursen, who had been suffering severe back pain since sustaining an injury on Bataan. He finally got the surgical relief he'd needed for three and a half years. Upon their arrival the former POWs filled out forms identifying themselves by name, rank, serial number, state of health, and who should be notified of their recovery. Next each was asked to fill out a five-page war crimes questionnaire. The first two pages were turned over to the special AGAS unit; the next two pages were given to the judge advocate general (JAG) team, which arrived later at the camp; and the final sheet was forwarded to Military Intelligence.

When asked if anyone had questioned them about visits by doctors from outside the camp or about suspicion they might have been subjected to medical experiments, all the Mukden survivors I questioned said no one on Recovery Team No. 1 or military personnel taking affidavits once they were back in the United States ever brought up the subject. It was many years later, beginning in the 1980s, that some former POWs began to connect the dots after media attention to the subject of Unit 731 activities and the unit's proximity to the Mukden camp.

Colonel Donovan reported that Col. James Gillespie, a medical doctor at the POW hospital, believed that the Japanese had thoroughly inoculated all prisoners against disease, although, of course, the serums used were unfamiliar to him and the other medical officers at the POW hospital.[4] Nevertheless, Recovery Team No. 1 set out to conduct a complete immunization of all former POWs, using vaccines that had been delivered for that purpose. The aim was to vaccinate POWs returning from Mukden against all possible contagious diseases they might be carrying. (Donovan noted that some former POWs had already been evacuated before all serums were available; the Navy was informed to continue the process.)

When B-29s began dropping large amounts of supplies, the "morale effect on the ex-prisoners was extremely good and perhaps this was more important than the supplies themselves," Donovan later recalled. As morale improved Donovan set a priority for evacuation: those with medical needs first (350 men) and then by age, oldest first. He was careful to avoid repeating the resentment that had swept through the American ranks when General Wainwright selected thirty-five POW officers who were to accompany him on his plane (probably the high-ranking American, British, and Dutch officers who had been with him in Hsian and those who had arrived at Mukden from Formosa the previous May). The colonel announced that he would not honor any more requests for officers to be evacuated by name except by direct order of necessity from General Wedemeyer. This move was appreciated by the men.

Another move very much appreciated was the arrival of a "well-traveled reporter from the CBI Roundup [a China-Burma-India Theater publication] named Master Sergeant Fred Friendly. His talks were universally popular with the ex-POWs who were universally hungry for war news and anecdotes of the type Sgt. Friendly had to offer."[5] An officer of the OSS team, 2nd Lt. Joseph Zalmanoff, translated Friendly's remarks into Russian and Chinese. Friendly, who later became an award-winning producer and president of CBS News, wrote his own account of his visit to Mukden for the CBI Roundup:

Manchuria POWs Generous Hosts to G.I. Rescuers

Mukden, Manchuria—Back in the dark days of 1942 when Bataan was hanging by a thread, there wasn't one of us "Stateside commandos" who didn't vow that if he ever met the veterans of Bataan, he'd give them his shirt, his last can of beer, and gladly shine their shoes.

But here at the Mukden prison camp we have found it virtually impossible to wait on these boys or in any way honor them as they deserve to be. I gave one squad of liberated POWs a bottle of Three Feathers [whiskey] that Bill Cavanaugh had given me back at Kunming. The boys took it and then presented me with half a case of Russian cognac. At chow time these soldiers won't eat their two eggs unless they give you three. If you try to wash your own dishes, a DSC [Distinguished Service Cross] wearer will grab them and tell you to sit down. If there is no seat at the movies, colonels who commanded divisions in the Philippines will offer you theirs—and be offended if you don't take it.

All of us who have come to Mukden agree that these are the most courteous, most generous bunch of Americans on the face of the globe. They can't do enough for you. And I think the reason is that for the first time in years they are free and are thrilled to be able to be with Yanks fortunate enough not to have suffered under the Japs.

These ex-prisoners are inclined to forget sometimes that they are not under Jap domination any longer and from force of habit bow a little when introduced and actually ask permission to speak to you. But in the last two weeks they have made enormous strides, with an improved diet including fruit salad, good coffee, eggs and other items so long denied them. They have gained as much as 20 pounds per man; that Yankee sparkle is coming back to their eyes. And one major even pulled his rank the other day, which is a damn good sign.

But the hairs that turned gray will never turn brown again; the narrow, painful-looking legs may never be strong again.

Magnificent Scene

There was one magnificent little scene enacted here the day after the liberation. The 14 B-29 men who had been isolated just outside the prison wall since their capture in December, were marched into the main prison yard. As they entered, the other prisoners stood and cheered. Then one sergeant, with one arm missing, rushed over to a Superfort pilot and greeted him with:

"Hi fellow. Welcome to the camp. It's good to see you."

The pilot replied, "Thanks, sarge. It's good to be with Yanks again. Sorry about your arm."

"Aw, dat's all right. I got it when the Superforts came over. It was some sight to see you boys", the sergeant said.

A sob broke loose from the big pilot's eyes and he could say nothing.

"Stop dat bawling!" the G.I. shouted. "Come on over, and I'll brew you up some good Stateside coffee."

Learns of Waves

An ex-Navy prisoner, Chief Petty officer Joe Davis, just about flipped his lid when we told him about the WAVES [Women Appointed for Volunteer Emergency Service] and that he'd have to salute lady officers.

"Listen, buddy, I've been in submarines for 20 years and I ain't ever gonna salute no female sailor", he replied. "I ain't going home till they get rid of them WAVES. How could they do this to me?"

I also met the man who drafted me in 1941: Col. Albert Christie who made history in the Philippines by refusing to surrender his unit even after the Wainwright surrender. He's quite a hero with the men here, but he was more interested in talking about the 1,500-man mess hall he'd built at Ft. Devens, Mass., than about Bataan.

Everybody is sweating out the trip home. But to some of them "home" is the Philippines or Hong Kong or Peiping, a lot of them being professional soldiers who haven't been in the States in three or four hitches. Everybody is looking better, feeling better and in another week will be in good enough shape to start griping in the greatest tradition of the American soldier.[6]

Master Sergeant Friendly remained at the Mukden camp until the last group of former prisoners was evacuated on board the hospital ship *Colbert* on September 13, 1945. As he stood on the pier at Dairen next to Colonel Donovan, the colonel turned to him and said, "Sergeant, you did a great job—for a Jew-boy." In later years Fred Friendly delighted in telling that anecdote to his family and colleagues at CBS News.[7]

In his introduction to his 1967 memoir, *Due to Circumstances Beyond Our Control . . .* , Friendly wrote that just three images from his coverage of World War II have stuck with him: "Hiroshima and Nagasaki just a few days after the first two atomic bombs had been dropped; the sight of the Bataan Death March survivors after their liberation from a prison camp in Mukden, Manchuria; and the liberation of the Mauthausen concentration camp in Austria are the only scars I bear from what was, for me, a relatively soft war."[8]

A total of 340 former POWs were evacuated by air between August 24 and September 10. Later, 105 civilians interned at the Mukden Club were also processed; many of them were missionaries who wished to remain to carry on their work in Manchuria.

On September 5 Colonel Donovan received a radio message stating that all former POWs would be required to sign "security certificates" to ensure that they would not release any information about their captivity unless authorized by the War Department. This distressed the colonel, because by that time 277 former POWs had already been evacuated by air. The AGAS delivered these certificates to the camp and then had to track down those individuals already evacuated. I was the first to bring the existence of these "security certificates," and the long-term consequences they had for some ex-POWs, to light.[9]

Former Mukden POW Pfc. Philip Haley still has a copy of this certificate, which could more accurately be described as a "gag order," which he signed on Guam. Its subject is "Publicity in connection with liberated Prisoners of War," and it instructs former POWs not to discuss anyone who assisted in escapes or special escape or intelligence activities within the camp. But the verbal caveats given to many returning former prisoners were much more threatening: they were told not to give newspaper or radio interviews or to discuss their captivity with others, even family members, unless authorized by the military, and that they could be subject to court-martial if they disobeyed this order. Apparently the order's main purpose was to tamp down on postwar anti-Japanese feeling.

Haley said he thought that the directions in this certificate applied mainly to press interviews, not to questions by medical doctors, that the restriction applied only while he was still in the military, and that he was no longer bound by it when he was discharged in April 1946.[10] But some former POWs took the order far more seriously, sometimes with tragic consequences. One former POW's wife said her husband burst into tears in a doctor's office years later, when the doctor persisted in asking if the man could think of any reason why he was experiencing certain ongoing health problems. "I was told I couldn't discuss those reasons," the man sobbed. The Mukden POW camp is the only camp where all former POWs were ordered to sign this certificate while still in camp

Philip Haley's copy of the "gag order" he signed on Guam, September 1945. Collection of Philip Haley.

(although as noted, some had left the camp before the order was issued). Many do not recall signing it at all; others remembered being told to sign it at some point on the way home, usually in Manila, Yokohama, or Guam.

While they were awaiting evacuation, the Mukden former prisoners were allowed out of the compound. Sgt. Charles Dragich said he was afraid to venture into Mukden City after a Russian soldier told him (Dragich was Rumanian and could understand Russian) that several former POWs had gone into Mukden City and disappeared, perhaps taken to Siberia. But many others did venture out—to a nearby brewery or just to walk the chaotic streets of Mukden. TSgt. Robert Rosendahl told of seeing many sick Chinese lying in gutters, dying. When he asked about them, he was told that they had been turned loose from a laboratory near Harbin (Unit 731). Later he realized that the dying Chinese he saw were part of the medical experiments that took place at Ping Fan.[11]

One former POW who was determined to scour Mukden for camera film was Pfc. Joseph Vater. He had traded a Japanese saber to an Air Force crewman for a Zeiss Ikon box camera. He brought some boots into Mukden City and sold them for money to buy film. After searching several shops he found a Chinese who had worked for American Tobacco Company and spoke perfect English. "What are you looking for?" he asked. The Chinese man then accompanied Vater to many shops until they found one that had thirteen rolls of film in stock. They fit the camera, and Vater proceeded to create a unique archive of postwar scenes at the Mukden camp: the cemetery, the buildings, former prisoners packed and ready to leave and on the train to Dairen, former prisoners on the hospital ship. He has donated his collection to the POW museum at the Brooke County Public Library in Wellsburg, West Virginia.[12]

Colonel Donovan had been ordered to turn over all Japanese camp personnel to the Russians, which he did on September 11. But Colonel Matsuda escaped from Russian custody and blended into the population in Mukden. He was spotted by former MKK factory manager Yoshio Kai, who then informed the OSS's SSgt. Hal Leith, who had returned to Mukden to take up residence at the Yamato Hotel and continue his surveillance of the Russians. Leith had Matsuda arrested and brought to the hotel. At first Matsuda denied who he was, but when Leith walked into the room, "Matsuda turned pale as a ghost."[13] Matsuda was subsequently put on trial in Shanghai, where he was sentenced to hard labor for seven years. (Captain Kuwashima, the camp doctor, was sentenced to death by hanging.)[14]

The first hospital ship, the *Relief*, arrived September 7 at Dairen to begin evacuating the remaining former POWs. The Russians interfered with communications, so Donovan had to fly to Dairen to make contact with the American commodore, C. C. Wood, who commanded the Naval fleet at Dairen. Two more hospital ships arrived the next day, the *Colbert* and *Louisville*. On September 12, 753 American, British, Australian, and Dutch former POWs left for Okinawa on the *Relief*, and 630 sailed the following day, September 13, on the *Colbert*. The *Colbert* got caught in a typhoon and hit a mine. Two sailors were killed in the engine room as a result of the explosion, and the ship had to be towed to Manila.

A member of the *Relief* crew wrote a description of the arrival of the former POWs to board his ship, late at night on September 11:

They were heard before they were seen. The dock itself was floodlighted. Beyond the dock was darkness. At 2050, the first of them stepped out of the darkness, into the glare of the dock floodlights, first one, then two, then ten, then the whole procession. They came in a mob, carrying all their worldly possessions on their backs or in duffel bags.

The entire ship's company manned the rail to greet them. As the ex-prisoners of war crowded the dock at the foot of the gangway, the ship's crew shouted over the rail to them, tossing them cigarettes, swapping stories, finding out where they were from "back in the States." The ship's Red Cross lights and green band had been illuminated, and someone had started Stateside music playing over the ship's public address system. . . . Dixie, the Marine Hymn, Stardust. The RELIEF was the first American ship these men had seen in three years; in some cases, four.

The first thing they wanted was a shower. They were provided with soap, towels and a clean soft bed. Then, after they had been made comfortable, a huge steak dinner was served. They had ice cream for dessert.

By midnight, most of them had gone to bed. . . . After everything was quiet, some of the ex-prisoners, hungry for conversation, or too excited to sleep, stayed about the decks, swapping yarns with the crew, or listening to accounts of what had been going on at home during the past four years. They wanted to know who the movie stars were, what songs were being sung; they listened proudly to descriptions of the rocket guns, and the accounts of Kwajalein, Okinawa, and Guam, and the others. . . . During the cruise, every attention was paid to the comfort and convenience of the passengers. Special entertainment programs were played over the ship's public address system; the Chaplains provided each passenger with all of the comforts the ship could afford them. News of the outside world was broadcast over the Crew's entertainment radios, direct from San Francisco. The ship's official communications equipment was kept on constant watch over specially designated circuits, waiting to intercept messages addressed to the ex-prisoners from their families. Each day the passengers were served ice cream and the ship's company donated a part of the welfare profits as personal credit in the ship's canteen and ship's store for each of the prisoners. And the men of the ship spent their off hours listening to the accounts of cruelty and brutality these returning heroes told, and swapping with them accounts of life at home, the history of the war, and the latest music and popular songs. Crew members sought out ex-prisoners from their home towns or states, and helped them to re-envisage what life would be like in the community to which they were returning.

Stories told by the ex-prisoners, of the treatment they had received at the hands of the Japanese, will live in the memories of the men of the RELIEF as first hand records of the infamy of the enemy they fought.[15]

Finally the evacuation of former POWs from Mukden was complete. They were on their way home at last. Some received a nicer welcome than others, and all were a bit apprehensive.

An eighteen-year-old English girl, Hilary Seymour-Cole, saw that apprehension and the imprint of memories not easily shaken as she stood on the pier at

Southampton, England, watching British former prisoners from Japanese camps disembark from the troop ship that had brought them home. Her poem, titled "A Salute," catches that mood:

I hear voices strangely young
Call across the alien sea.
Unheralded, unsung,
Strange they feel, returning free.
Oddly dim, the years behind
Fade into oblivion—
As with thankful heart and mind,
Each awaits reunion.[16]

Many former POWs had joyful, tearful reunions with their families at docksides, railroad stations, on the grounds of Letterman General Hospital outside San Francisco, or by just quietly walking in the back door. For some, though, their first experience arriving on U.S. soil was decidedly a jolt. SSgt. Art Campbell arrived in Seattle and at least was processed by a team of civil, if somewhat crisp, screeners whose job it was to create a full service record for these returning former prisoners, who often arrived back in the States with no paperwork. That was their first roadblock: for many, future medical care at Veterans Administration hospitals hinged on what they could remember about injury or illness to tell the screeners. Campbell was chatting with a buddy when a young woman sitting behind the desk interrupted him, saying, "You can finish your conversation later. We have to complete your paperwork now." Campbell reached over, lifted her

Former POWs on board hospital ship *Relief*, September 1945. Photo by Joseph A. Vater.

up by her shoulders until she was at eye level, and said, "Ma'am, you can complete your paperwork when we've finished our conversation, all right?" "Okay," she answered. She later became his wife. Staff Sergeant Campbell was ordered to report to the hospital in Van Nuys, California. There the Medical Corps took away all the former POWs' clothing in order to keep them confined. Campbell said he was asked no direct questions about his time in Mukden.

General Wainwright heard that some of "his boys" were at Van Nuys, so he stopped in for a visit. The medical team would not let him enter the ward until he removed all his clothes, which he did. Once inside the general identified himself and demanded that the men be given their clothing.[17]

Pvt. Ken Towery wrote about the frustrations of his railroad trip back home to Texas after arriving in San Francisco. It had been bizarre enough, after he was lucky enough to secure a pass from Letterman General Hospital to visit the city, to encounter a security guard at the gate who was an Italian former POW just released from a U.S. POW camp. But as he noted, what was to follow was worse still. Finally Towery and his Texas friends were boarded on a train bound for Fort Sam Houston in San Antonio. Their joy turned to horror when the railroad cars were locked and sealed shut. Everywhere the train stopped along the way, crowds would be there, waving, shouting, blowing kisses.

"But there was no touching," Towery wrote. "It was heart-rending, traumatic. One wanted so much to be among them. To this day I have never understood the logic of the sealed cars."[18] At San Antonio, Towery recalled, "we went to a guarded area, then in single file and under orders not to break rank for any reason, to barrack quarters prepared for us. The line was guarded by soldiers spaced at intervals. Their job was to prevent gathered family members from disrupting the proceedings. They were not always successful."[19]

Towery was placed under quarantine in Brooke Army Hospital because shadows had been found on his lungs and the doctors wanted to make sure he didn't have tuberculosis. After much protest, he was given a short leave to go home. He spent several more months at Brooke, being treated for parasites, until his discharge in July 1946. But since the physicians could find no proof he had a contagious disease, Towery felt they were acting "somewhat arbitrarily." For all the trauma surrounding his homecoming, that is probably an understatement.

But the most egregious homecoming may have been experienced by Pvt. Walter Middleton and his friends, a small group of North Carolina mountain boys who had survived Bataan, Cabanatuan, the *Tottori Maru*, and Mukden together. When they got to San Francisco, a woman who had somehow found employment with the military as a screener asked Walter and his friends where they had served in the military. "We were prisoners of war," they replied. "Oh!" she exclaimed. "What if we had all thrown up our hands and surrendered? We'd all be speaking Japanese!"[20]

Furious at her insensitivity, but also feeling constrained by the "gag order" they had signed in Manila, with its caveat not to discuss their captivity with anyone, the group of former POWs clammed up and refused to answer any questions put to them. "Some doctors tried to debrief us, but we didn't cooperate with them," Middleton recalled.[21] They were put on a train to North Carolina, but instead of joyful reunions with families, they were taken to Moore General Hospital in Swannanoa, North Carolina, where they were locked in a room with padded walls. After about two weeks, one of them was able to make contact with their U.S. congressman, who quickly arranged for better treatment.

Middleton remained at Moore Hospital for several months, being treated for the lingering amoebic dysentery that had plagued him during nearly his entire captivity at Mukden. He received an honorable discharge with a "Certificate of Disability" and was discharged from the hospital in October 1946. Middleton noted that his discharge contained a "partial" service record, with no mention of Bataan or Mukden. "Fear is one of the worst things to get rid of," he remarked. "I had nightmares for years until I wrote my memoir. I've been able to help a few veterans to talk about their experience."[22]

Suffice it to say that no former POW who survived the prolonged malnutrition and injuries of Japanese captivity ever fully regained his prewar health. As Mukden medic Robert Brown observed, "We all have aeschemic heart disease, from malnutrition."[23] In varying degrees, former POWs of the Pacific war have been plagued by arthritis, diminished eyesight, digestive problems, bouts of malaria and other tropical diseases, and recurring ailments that for some are not properly identified or treated—to say nothing of post-traumatic stress disorder, which was not even a recognized condition in the immediate postwar years and from which all suffered periodically.

As mentioned earlier, one of the biggest roadblocks to effective postwar treatment for these men was incomplete medical records—or no medical records at all. Many say it has taken them fifty years to be granted the percentage of disability payments they should have been receiving because the recognition of captivity-related symptoms has been agonizingly slow within the Veterans Administration (VA) system.

For example, Wake Island civilian Joseph Astarita, a former POW, described the frustration of trying to convince an "intake" physician at a Florida VA hospital that he was suffering from frostbite in his toes. "Where were you in captivity?" the doctor asked him. Astarita told him that he was, the first year in Woosung, China. "Oh no," said the doctor. "China is warm—coolie hats." Astarita, an accomplished artist, said he regretted not having brought along his sketch of the water tower in Woosung, completely encased in ice during the winter of 1942.[24]

The late Melvin Routt, a past national commander of the American Defenders of Bataan and Corregidor (ADBC), spent many years working with the staff at Letterman General Hospital to acquaint them with some captivity-related illnesses. Routt, who was a fireman first class on the submarine tender USS *Canopus*, was sent to Mitsui's huge Omuta coal mine at Fukuoka, Japan, along with 890 other Americans. They were fortunate enough to have a doctor among them, Thomas Hewlett, who kept a detailed record of the diminishing calorie intake for the prisoners and the long-term medical consequences of malnutrition. Hewlett spent many hours compiling data for the VA, noting, for example, that the standard caloric requirement for a man in his twenties doing "moderate labor" is 2,800 calories, but for Americans working in the Omuta mine, the daily intake had been reduced to just 485 calories by 1945. Most POWs lost between eighty and one hundred pounds in Japanese captivity.

Routt helped the Letterman staff identify many captivity-related conditions needing ongoing treatment and set up a system for sharing the data with other hospitals in the VA system. Many of his fellow former POWs around the country have done the same at their local VA hospitals. But at every gathering of the ADBC, another handful of former POWs learn about the latest conditions identified for which they can, belatedly, apply to receive disability benefits. Some do not live long enough to see an increase in their monthly disability allowance. For them, time has run out.

13

Justice in the Aftermath?

When the Admiral Nimitz National Museum of the Pacific War convened a symposium on the Tokyo War Crimes Trials at Fredericksburg, Texas, in October 1996, former State Department spokesman Hodding Carter III summed up the trials by calling them the "dog that did not bark." Indeed, many historians, scholars, reporters, and military participants view the 1946–48 trials as tedious, dragging on for so long that newspaper coverages slipped to the back pages and some newspapers discontinued coverage altogether.

Two major criticisms of the Tokyo trials persist. First, Emperor Hirohito was not put on trial—at the urging of Gen. Douglas MacArthur, who warned of virtual anarchy among the Japanese people if their deified emperor were put on the witness stand. In a June 1946 interview chief U.S. prosecutor Joseph Keenan told the *New York Times* that "higher political circles" had decided against trying the emperor as a war criminal.[1] As a result the Japanese people avoided the collective guilt so deeply ingrained in the German people, because in their eyes their emperor had been exonerated.

The second lingering criticism of the Tokyo trials is that General Shiro Ishii, who developed the biological warfare program that centered at his laboratory in Ping Fan, Manchuria, known internally as Unit 731, was detained but not tried for his hideous experiments on living humans. Scholars have noted the irony in the fact that Ishii's counterpart in Nazi Germany, Dr. Josef Mengele, was arduously sought but escaped detection at a series of displaced persons camps after the war ended in Europe and managed to escape to Brazil, where he later died by drowning. By contrast, after faking his own funeral, General Ishii was discovered and detained under house arrest but cleverly manipulated American investigators by never admitting that his experiments included American prisoners of war and successfully concealing the paperwork on his medical team's visits to the Mukden camp by burying those reports on the grounds of his family's estate in Chiba prefecture, outside Tokyo City.[2]

Colonel Tomorado Masada, M.D., second in command to General Ishii at Ping Fan, gave information to U.S. investigator Murray Sanders that Ishii's biological warfare project there was forbidden by the emperor, so Ishii made his project a subsidiary of the Water Purification Project and gave his program the name Anti-Epidemic Water Supply Unit.[3]

Ishii offered to give the Americans his tissue slides of experiments on Chinese prisoners in exchange for immunity from prosecution. Apparently some scientists thought the slides would be of considerable value. (The slides later proved to be of minimal value, due primarily to faulty methodology, and may have been discarded. In any event, they apparently have gone missing from the laboratory at Fort Detrick, Maryland, where they were supposed to have been stored.) Because Ishii's aides at Ping Fan had confessed to their Soviet captors about human experimentation, the Russians urgently wanted to cross-examine the general on the witness stand. Cold War fears that the Soviets might glean enough of Ishii's data to conduct biological warfare on the United States prompted American prosecutors to agree that allowing Ishii to give such data at trial was not worth the risk.[4]

Of more interest to the 36,260 Americans[5] confined to Japanese military prison camps and company work sites, and to the families of those who did not return, was the release by General MacArthur in April 1946 of the CEOs of the two largest users of Allied prisoner labor: Kiyoshi Goko, chairman of Mitsubishi, and Suhin Ikeda, managing director of Mitsui. Both had been detained, along with other members of the *zaibatsu* (cartel of leading Japanese corporations) as "suspected war criminals" in December 1945, but since all said they had followed the August 20, 1945, directive to destroy "documents which would be unfavorable to us in the hands of the enemy,"[6] no paper trail could firmly be established to prove that company executives were directly involved in the planning and prosecution of the war, which were the criteria for Class A prosecutions at the trials. But at least one prosecutor, Robert Donihi, said he believed the *zaibatsu* chiefs "could have and should have" been prosecuted at the Class B and C trials, which took place at Yokohama, for mistreatment of prisoners of war.[7]

For Mukden former POWs, one Yokohama prosecution offered some degree of satisfaction. Several had the opportunity to give affidavits at the trial of one of the most brutal members of the camp staff, Corporal Eichi Noda, when his trial began September 19, 1947. TSgt. Harry Simmons testified that Noda beat SSgt. Fred Anderson so badly that the sergeant became unconscious and beat Sgt. James Delanty so severely that the prisoner went insane. "It was the most brutal thing I have ever seen," Simmons testified.[8] Simmons also testified that Noda had participated in the beating and deaths of the three Mukden escapees—Sergeant Chastain, Corporal Paliotto, and Seaman Meringolo. Simmons testified that he saw Noda beating one of the two smaller prisoners with a stick: "One of these boys had evidently been hit so hard that he dropped down on his hands and knees kind of like a dog; and he [Noda] was beating him around the head, shoulders and across the back."[9]

Their return to camp was no secret. Pvt. Christopher Vissaris saw the three prisoners after they had been recaptured and returned to the camp, and noted that "they were in a horrible condition."[10] Still others, including Sgt. James Baldassare, saw the three being brought back to the camp: "At this time Noda and one of the guards approached the three men. Each had a round club in his hand about 30 inches long and one and a half inches in diameter. Noda and the guard then proceeded to beat the three prisoners unmercifully with the clubs. They struck them across the face, on the head and on every part of the body. All of them stayed on their feet throughout the beating, which lasted for five or ten minutes."[11]

Even those who remained behind did not escape punishment. Sgt. George Johnston, who lived in the same barrack as one of the men who tried to break out testified that he was confined for ninety days in the guard house and after his release Corporal Noda beat him with clubs and a rock.[12] When Noda was not beating them with rocks and sticks, he lashed them with his tongue, "cuss[ing] and call[ing] us 'pigs' every time he came into camp," according to Cpl. Carl Donning.[14] Sgt. Baldassare further testified that "[Cpl.] Noda would slap American prisoners as they stood in line, and when they fell to the ground, he would say: 'Get up, you yellow, white son of a bitch,' and 'that's for my folks in Frisco.' He used any excuse, like infraction of rules he made up on the spot. Noda was alone in doing the beatings and no superior ordered him."[13] Indeed, Noda never missed an opportunity to remind the American POWs of their captors' superiority. In the end, however, it was Noda himself who submitted to a higher authority. On October 14, 1947, with two and a half months of his sentence "remitted due to confinement" (reduced to time already served). Like most other Japanese convicted of war crimes, he did not serve his full sentence.

The day after the Class A verdicts were announced in Tokyo in November 1948, General MacArthur released nineteen detained Class A suspected criminals, none of whom had been indicted or tried. By the time the peace treaty went into effect in February 1952, the general, with the approval of the White House, had released 892 detainees, at the request of the Japanese government. President Dwight D. Eisenhower later expedited the release of Class B and C criminals, such as Corporal Noda, in 1957, and by the end of 1958, the Sugamo Prison was empty. The Japanese Diet paid the back salaries and restored the pensions of those who had been released.

In contrast to the Tokyo trials, the Shanghai trials, convened by China Command general Albert Wedemeyer and taking place at the Ward Road Jail beginning February 28, 1946, were far more efficient. For example, Lieutenant (now Captain) Toru Miki, who had ordered and participated in numerous acts of brutality, was sentenced on March 14, 1946, to twenty-five years at hard labor. Like Noda, however, he did not serve his full sentence. Colonel Genji Matsuda's trial began January 18, 1947. He was sentenced to seven years at hard labor because the tribunal found that no witnesses testified the colonel had directly participated in mistreatment of prisoners or caused their deaths. Unlike his peers, however, POW hospital chief Captain Joichi Kuwashima was sentenced to death by hanging because numerous Mukden former POWs testified to witnessing the beatings he had personally administered, his brutality in sending sick prisoners to work in the MKK factory, and his direct responsibility for the deaths of several prisoners.[15]

To the dismay of many Mukden survivors, other notorious abusers on the camp staff, such as Captain Ishikawa, Lieutenant Mura, Lieutenant Ando, and Sergeant Meajima, were not apprehended and thus evaded prosecution. At least at Shanghai, with the hanging of Kuwashima, the dog barked a little. But where justice has not been served is in the postwar lives of former POWs of the Pacific war. Unlike military POWs confined in Nazi *stalags,* the Pacific POWs have not had the satisfaction of seeing an entire nation's government, corporations, and citizens pay billions in compensation to its victims or feel a sense of collective guilt.

Whereas our State Department actively supported efforts to force compensation payments from the German government and corporations, as well as Swiss banks, similar legal moves toward the Japanese government and its corporations have met with active interference by the State Department. In the German cases our State Department declined to file a "Statement of Interest" with the courts, but when lawsuits were filed against Japanese corporations by former POW slave laborers for compensation, the State Department filed a Statement of Interest with California courts willing to hear such cases in 1999–2001, citing jeopardy to our foreign relations with Japan. As lead attorney David Casey said of the California cases, the State Department filing forced the courts to defer to our government. He summed up the outcome: "The State Department could have declined to file a Statement of Interest and allowed the courts to interpret the 1951 Treaty of Peace without its intervention. Had that occurred, on the merits [of their cases] the POWs would have won, allowing the world's greatest judicial system to work, without political interference."[16] The Supreme Court declined to hear attorney Casey's appeal.

Faced with a dead end in the courts, former POWs of the Pacific war have turned to Congress in hopes of gaining an ex gratia payment similar to the twenty thousand dollars authorized in 1988 by Congress to be given to each American of Japanese descent interned in the United States during World War II (none of whom performed slave labor or died from starvation or beatings; they were interned only after the Japanese had rounded up every white man, woman, and child in Asia and thrown them into prisons or internment camps).[17] Several bills have been introduced in recent years, only to be deleted by the House-Senate

Conference Committee at the request of the White House or by the insistence of a senator with his own agenda. So far Congress has made just two payments to our former prisoners of the Japanese: $1.00 per day of captivity for "missed meals" (War Claims Act of 1948) and, later, $1.50 per day of captivity for "pain and suffering and forced labor" (War Claims Act of 1952). In recent years the governments of Great Britain, the Netherlands, Canada, Australia, New Zealand, Norway, and even the Isle of Man have offered their citizens who suffered in Japanese captivity a one-time payment of between twenty and twenty-four thousand dollars. Alone among the Allied nations, the United States has not done so.

At a September 2001 symposium in San Francisco held in commemoration of the fiftieth anniversary of the signing of the Treaty of Peace with Japan, I challenged the former ambassador to Japan, Thomas Foley, to explain our government's position on this matter. "It's up to Congress," he replied. "If Congress thinks our government hasn't done enough for our prisoners of war, Congress can do more."[18] Similarly, no effort toward compensation for former prisoners of war has been made by the Japanese government or corporations because our State Department has not requested such gestures—in marked contrast to its strong stance toward the German government.

The dwindling number of survivors of Japanese captivity can only hope that a new administration in the White House will not block new congressional initiatives, but none is holding his breath. "They're all just waiting until we die off, and then the problem will go away," some say sadly.

Back in Time

Over the years a few Mukden camp survivors have traveled to Mukden
City (now Shenyang, which means "Opinion of the Gods") hoping to
be directed to the outskirts of the city, where the camp was located,
and to see the MKK factory where they toiled for over three years. But local
officials seemed to have no idea where to send them. Then, in the early 1990s,
Jing Yang, a native of Shenyang and now a professor of history at Shenyang
University, discovered the remnants of the camp site, now in the Daodong district of Shenyang City. Two of the three camp barracks were still standing; they
had been converted to government-subsidized low income housing. The POW
hospital was now an old-age home. Part of the camp's high wall was still there,
as was the electric power transmission tower. And the MKK factory, now jointly
owned by Chinese and Czech entrepreneurs, was still there, renamed Zhang
Chi Friendship Factory.

Another Shenyang native, Ao Wang, now living in North Carolina, heard of
Yang's discovery, and on one of his frequent trips back home, Wang sought out
Yang and local television producer-writer Bing Zhang, who had begun highlight-
ing the discovery of the camp site in 1992. Wang began to dream of turning the
remaining structures of the camp into a museum, as a reminder of World War II
Chinese-American friendship and of the brutal Japanese occupation that forged
that friendship. The combined efforts of Yang, Zhang, and Wang made local officials aware of this bit of history in their midst. But the idea of a museum at the
site languished until September 2003, when an expedition of former POWs and
Chinese American activists visited Shenyang and the camp site.

Wang had spent over a year planning the trip with the help of the
Washington, D.C.–based Truth Council for World War II in Asia. He attended
the spring 2003 reunion of the American Defenders of Bataan and Corregidor
and sought out Mukden survivors, hoping to interest them in joining the expedition. Some shared former Pfc. Joseph Vater's reaction: "Why would *anyone*
want to go back? I spent the worst three years of my life there!" But eventually

six former POWs expressed interest. Three backed out due to poor health, and another canceled at the last minute. But Pfc. Oliver "Red" Allen and TSgt. Robert Rosendahl began making plans to go to Shenyang the following September. I joined the expedition. When contacted, *New York Times* Beijing bureau chief Joseph Kahn agreed with me that this would be a story worth covering and pledged to send a correspondent and cameraman to meet us in Shenyang on September 17.

When eighty-two-year-old Oliver Allen stepped to the door of the airplane that had brought him from Los Angeles to the sparkling new airport at Shenyang, China, on September 16, 2003, he saw a crowd of Chinese reporters, photographers, and television cameramen on the tarmac. Allen, a gregarious retired Texas school administrator, was puzzled. "I looked around to see who the celebrities were on our flight," he recalled, "and then I realized it was *us!*" Allen and his wife Mildred were joined by fellow former POW Robert Rosendahl, eighty-two, also retired after a career in military and Justice Department posts, and his wife Bettye. Nearly sixty-one years after they had stumbled as prisoners of war off a dingy train at the railroad station across town, they were back in Mukden. These two survivors of the Mukden POW camp were about to get a red-carpet welcome as they returned to the place where they had slaved, shivered, and starved for nearly three years as prisoners of the Japanese from 1942 to 1945.

Also accompanying Allen and Rosendahl was former SSgt. Hal Leith, one of the OSS paratroopers who had rescued the POWs on August 16, 1945, just ahead of advancing Russian troops. Leith, eighty-four, was with his wife Helen. All six had agreed to join a delegation of Chinese Americans on this special journey back in time. Over the next few days Allen, Rosendahl, and Leith would be escorted everywhere, be honored guests at the American Consulate, participate in two press conferences, visit the local museum, submit to hours of interviews by local media, and, most important, walk through the barracks where Allen and Rosendahl lived and the factories where they were forced to work for Mitsubishi and its subsidiary companies.

"The nightmares are lessening now," Allen confided three days into the visit. "So far, the only thing that hurt me here was going into that museum." He was referring to the 9-18 Museum, named for the date, September 18, 1931, when Japanese troops parachuted into Mukden and began their occupation of China. Built around remnants of the railroad station, which Japanese forces destroyed, the museum houses room after huge room of artifacts, exhibits, paintings, dioramas, and photos depicting the brutality of Japanese rule and the stubborn resistance of Chinese guerrilla forces. But the displays were all too much for Allen. "There was so much atrocity, I couldn't take it all. I lived through so much of it—I had to stop." Allen and his wife left the museum early and waited outside for the others.

The next morning, September 18, 2003, brought the moment Allen, Rosendahl, and Leith had been waiting for. Accompanied by Chinese officials, tour organizers, a crush of Chinese reporters, photographers, and video cameramen, along with correspondent Jim Yardley and cameraman Doug Kanter from the *New York Times,* the former prisoners and their rescuer returned to the spot they had last seen fifty-eight years earlier: the Mukden POW camp, barracks and still-operating MKK factory.

Shenyang has been rebuilt and greatly expanded since 1945, so its outskirts surround the old gate and electrical tower that mark the camp's entrance. Local officials, who accompanied the group of Americans everywhere, watching Allen and Rosendahl point out their barracks (now low-income housing), the gate, tower, and original equipment still within the factory, realized that this site represents the last remnants of Japan's wartime occupation of the region.

Allen and Rosendahl recognized the MKK factory right away, along with several nearby buildings when they spotted them. Standing just inside the entrance at the factory, the former POWs recalled with considerable pride how they had sabotaged every stage of the construction of this huge tool and die factory the prisoners had been forced to build, primarily to produce aircraft parts for Mitsubishi's Zero fighter planes. "This concrete floor," Rosendahl said, pointing downward, "we buried so many tools, shovels, gears, anything we could, every time we had to pour this concrete. One day," he chuckled, "we buried a whole lathe while the guards were at lunch!" Then he turned to Allen and pointed up. "See? The big overhead cranes are still there, and these columns. The walls are the same, but the ceiling is new." Allen nodded.

The factory was surrounded by a paved walkway and road, but the terrain changed abruptly as Allen and Rosendahl walked toward the two remaining barracks that had housed American POWs. Suddenly the group was picking its way along a dirt path, pitted with mud holes, past tiny yards and flimsy dwellings. Their former barracks had been converted to small, one-room cubicles for the area's poorest residents. Entering the darkened building (there were no lights in the halls), Rosendahl said softly, "I remember these steps," as he climbed slowly to the second floor.

When the former POWs asked to see inside one of the rooms, a Chinese man rushed forward with a bunch of keys and, without knocking, unlocked a door. A startled woman about forty-five years of age jumped from her tiny bed, which nearly filled the room, furnished only with a black-and-white television, a chair, and a small bureau. She stood stiffly at attention, smiling hesitantly, while a crush of reporters and photographers jostled to view her space.

"Recognize any of this?" Rosendahl jokingly asked Allen. "Not this TV," Allen answered. Both men laughed, and they said no more of what they did remember about trying to stay alive in this place for nearly three years.

As the group was leaving the former POW barracks, two Chinese district officials in business suits approached *New York Times* correspondent Yardley and cameraman Kanter. Regional officials were aware that local press would be covering the POW visit, they explained, but they had *not* been informed that anyone from the *New York Times* would be there, questioning people, and they asked the two journalists to leave. Yardley quietly put away his notebook and suddenly the two buses carrying the POW entourage had a police escort leaving the site.

As we were leaving the site, I walked ahead of the group. A woman on her bicycle approached, shook hands, and withdrew from her basket a prized possession: a Bible. As we were admiring the big gold letters on the cover, two men in dark suits approached the woman and spoke abruptly to her. Quickly, she replaced the Bible in its bag and pedaled away, without a word. Freedom of religion is apparently still a work in progress in China.

Later that day, at a press conference in their hotel, Allen, Rosendahl, and Leith spoke of their days at Mukden and answered reporters' questions. Leith said he was grateful to have been able to save the POWs and to make sure they were in American custody before the Russians arrived. Rosendahl said he appreciated the enthusiasm of everyone who made this trip possible. But standing to speak, he said, "I can't possibly condense three and a half years in a few moments. I spent fifty-eight years trying to forget it all, so it's hard to remember."

Allen was still marveling at the crowd that had greeted the group's arrival at the airport. "It was the most touching experience," he said, "to know that people still care about what happened [to the former POWs] at Mukden. I had no idea the Chinese people are so interested in World War II POWs." When asked by a Chinese reporter if they knew of the germ warfare experiments that had occurred in the area, and whether they themselves had had any encounters with Japanese doctors, Rosendahl answered, "We were inoculated three different times. We were marched through the barber shop [to receive the inoculations]. We were told the shots were for hepatitis. We didn't know what it was for until after the war. In Mukden [City] I met a young medical student who wanted to practice his English. I noticed about twenty Chinese men dying on the streets. The student said, 'They're from north of here.' That's all I know." (The infamous biowarfare laboratory, Unit 731, was headquartered near Harbin, about 350 miles north of Mukden.)

Earlier, at the POW camp site, Rosendahl and Allen had an exchange that illustrated the ambivalence still surrounding the issue of Japanese medical experiments on U.S. POWs. Standing at the spot where the barber shop had been, Rosendahl turned to Allen and said, "Here's where the barbershop was." Allen nodded. "You remember," Rosendahl continued, "we walked through the barber shop to get our shots." Allen answered, "I never got any shots here." Rosendahl countered, "Sure, you remember, we went through the barber shop to get those shots." Allen replied, somewhat testily, "Look, I'd remember if I got any shots, and I never got any shots here at Mukden except from our people, after we were liberated." The answer to this contradiction is that only *some* of the POWs at Mukden were selected for treatment by visiting Japanese medical teams, but the understandably differing recollections of former POWs from this camp has led to much confusion over the past half century.

A highlight of the press conference, which lasted all afternoon, was when several elderly Chinese were introduced. They had worked alongside the POWs at the MKK factory, and some had only recently retired. One, Li-Shiu Lee, knew one POW only by the number pinned to his factory uniform: 266. "He gave me the first piece of chocolate I ever tasted, and I've always wanted to thank him," Lee said through an interpreter. I had heard of Lee's recollection, and I brought a message from POW 266, Neil Gagliano, to Lee. It read, "I was happy to hear from someone who had memories of that time beside me. Please tell Mr. Lee I said hello. I remembered giving him the chocolate. I'm glad to hear he's OK and still working. I indeed was POW 266 so long ago, but still only like yesterday. . . . God Bless you all and again thank you so very much. Yours truly, Neil Gagliano."[1] Lee's wrinkled face beamed as Gagliano's words were translated for him.

Former MKK worker Decun Gao also spoke, his voice shaking at the memories, about being blamed for giving the map to the escapees, about his ten-year imprisonment and torture by the Japanese, and about the death of his infant son from starvation. He became so overwhelmed with emotion that his wife had to finish telling the story.

September 18 is a very important date in China, especially in Shenyang, where the Japanese occupation began that night in 1931. A solemn observance takes place each year at night in the huge plaza in front of the 9-18 Museum. Oliver Allen and Hal Leith were too tired to attend the ceremonies, but with the aid of a wheelchair, Bob Rosendahl was taken to a place of honor in the front row, while thousands of local citizens, students, cadets, soldiers, and officials assembled quietly in the crisp night air.

Everyone stood silently until shortly after 9:00 P.M., when a huge temple gong sounded and sirens blared throughout the city for several minutes to mark the exact time when Japanese paratroops dropped from the sky, blew up the railroad station, and began fourteen years of brutal occupation. After the speeches, a throng of voices joined in singing the national anthem and a chorus of "Chee-na! Chee-na!" echoed from the plaza walls.

The next morning, September 19, while the former POWs and their wives went shopping, a small number of the visiting group, accompanied by a few journalists, were driven to the China Medical University, founded in 1929 and operated from 1931 to 1945 as a Japanese army medical college. A visiting professor of microbiology, Zhou Zheng Rin, has extensively researched Japan's wartime activities at the medical center, with special focus on the links between experiments developed here and the infamous biowarfare laboratories at Ping Fan. He made a detailed presentation to the group, noting that the chief of microbiology at this medical university during the 1930s was Dr. Masaji Kitano, who in 1941 replaced Dr. Shiro Ishii as head of Unit 731. Kitano received international attention for developing a vaccine for German measles, which he accomplished by experimenting extensively not only on animals but also on hundreds of local Chinese prisoners. He trained many students at the university hospital, who later transferred to Unit 731 to continue experimenting on Chinese and Russian prisoners, according to Professor Rin.

The visitors had hoped to gain some precise data on several American POWs who were brought to this hospital from the Mukden POW camp for treatment and surgery. A few prisoners returned to the camp alive, but many died here in the hospital. Rin dashed these hopes by revealing that, unfortunately, the Japanese had burned all relevant records in 1945, prior to surrendering, so no information on the POWs was apparently preserved. Rin asked if the visitors would like to see Kitano's underground laboratory, the entrance to which remains undisturbed in the middle of the medical university courtyard. It is usually off limits to visitors, but an exception was made on this day.

Descending the pitch-dark stone steps into this series of dirt-floored rooms was like going into an Egyptian tomb. A single bare bulb dangled from an overhead cord in an adjacent room, providing the only light as visitors viewed the dust-coated urns and jars and rusted animal cages that rested on a series of shelves around the room. But the unforgettable focal point of this subterranean chamber was the shrine Kitano had erected to honor the memory of all the animals whose lives had been sacrificed for his experiments—not the hundreds of humans who had perished here, only the four-footed rodents were memorialized in this spot.

On September 20, 2003, as the group was preparing for their final evening and a banquet to thank their Chinese hosts and journalists, Oliver Allen said he couldn't get over how built up the city he remembered as Mukden had become and how Shenyang had grown out to encompass the spot, isolated from the city, which had been their prison camp. But what still overwhelmed him was discovering time after time "how many people care about what happened to us here so long ago." It was such an unexpected contrast to that chilly day in November 1942, when Allen, Rosendahl, and their comrades first saw Mukden, Manchuria.

Jim Yardley's article was published September 19, 2003, in the *New York Times*. Simultaneously, local media coverage of the visiting Americans and their meetings with local Chinese had been extensively covered. But when the visit got international coverage through the *Times* story, it only took about two weeks for local Chinese officials to reconsider their reluctance to create a museum at

Dr. Masaji Kitano's shrine to sacrificed animals, China Medical University, 2003. Author photo.

Restored barrack interior, Mukden, 2006. Photo by Pat Wang.

the site. On October 8, 2003, China's Xinhua news agency carried this news on its wire service: "A prisoner-of-war (POW) camp used by Japanese invaders during World War II in Shenyang, capital of northeast China's Lianoning Province, is to be protected as a historical site, local authorities said. . . . The camp is one of the few existing sites in Shenyang testifying to Japanese war crimes, so historians believe it is of great significance to preserve the camp."[2]

Several years later, when the American Defenders of Bataan and Corregidor gathered for their annual reunion in Phoenix, Arizona, in May 2006, the Mukden survivors among them were greeted by Vice Director Ying Zhang of the Shenyang Municipality Cultural Heritage Bureau and members of his staff, who had flown from Shenyang to present slides and a memorial album to the survivors and their families, showing them the progress to date in restoring the remaining structures of the Mukden POW camp site. Oliver Allen wasn't well enough to travel to Phoenix, but Bob Rosendahl and his wife Bettye were there, along with Mukden survivors Charles Dragich, Elvin "Dave" Davis, and Robert Vogler. Museum officials explained that they have identified the perimeter of the camp site, including part of the high wall that surrounded it; the building that had been the POW hospital; the laundry; the water tower and boiler chimney; the remaining two of three barracks, now restored after occupants were relocated; and the former Japanese headquarters, which is being used as the museum containing photos, artifacts, and text about the POW experience at Mukden. Only buildings that remain are being restored; no attempt has been made to re-create what has already disappeared.

The officials were anxious to learn from the former POWs whether details of their restoration of one of the barracks was accurate. Rosendahl said, "Get rid of the light fixture; we only had one bare bulb to light our barracks." When shown the bath house, Rosendahl noted it was "rarely" used by the POWs. Davis went a step further and said flatly, "We only got to use it once, on Christmas Day in 1944." Vogler proudly announced that he was one of the 150 "troublemakers" (expert saboteurs) removed from Mukden and shipped to Mitsui's lead mine at Kamioka, Japan, in June 1944.

A sign in three languages, Chinese, Japanese, and English, has been erected at the entrance to the Mukden camp site, identifying it as the "WWII Allies POW Shenyang Concentration Camp and Memorial Museum." Officials hope that in the coming years, additional artifacts, diaries, and other memorabilia will be added to the already substantial collection, which is set off by a bronze bas-relief depicting the Bataan Death March—for so many Mukden POWs the deadly prelude to their years in Manchuria. Since that time the provincial Lianoning government has provided the equivalent of about seven million U.S. dollars to expand the museum even further, according to Ao and Pat Wang, who have formed a

Mukden survivors organization, the Mukden POW Remembrance Society, to act as liaison between the former POWs and the Shenyang museum officials.

On Memorial Day weekend 2006, the Shenyang museum officials traveled to New York City, where they conducted another presentation at the Overseas Press Club for Mukden former POW John Zenda and Catherine Meringolo Quoma, sister of one of the POW escapees executed in July 1943. Members of the American and Chinese press, as well as historians, scholars, and local members of the Chinese community who are working to preserve the history of World War II in Asia, also attended the event. Zenda told the officials, "I'm so glad you are preserving our camp as a reminder. Mitsubishi would have you believe these things didn't exist, but I know they did; I was *there*. You're doing the right thing." He added, "The Mukden camp was a horrible place to be. It was a prison within a prison if you did something wrong. I was interrogated for hours and put in isolation because I found some Chinese money on the ground and put it in my pocket."[3]

Sixty years on, the remaining Mukden survivors can take some comfort in knowing that people in the city of their former captivity are creating a museum that will tell at least some of the story, for future generations, of how Allied POWs suffered there so many years ago.

Epilogue

I hope this book will provide some definitive answers, at long last, to the controversy and confusion that have surrounded the question of whether some prisoners at Mukden were experimented upon by Japanese doctors who visited the camp on several occasions. We can now say with considerable certainty that the medical teams that visited the camp in February, April, and June 1943 were, indeed, from the biowarfare laboratory at Ping Fan, Unit 731, and that they did select some American POWs to receive certain toxins by inhalation, ingestion, or injection in order to determine their level of reaction and/or the dosage needed for effective infection. But exactly what toxins were used, and for what purpose, is a question that may never be fully answered—unless, that is, some Japanese authorities undertake to overturn the soil throughout the grounds of the Ishii family estate in order to find the medical data General Shiro Ishii ordered buried there in 1945—an event that is not likely to occur.

The question of medical experimentation on American POWs has vexed not only scholars and historians but also members of congressional committees and the leadership of the American Defenders of Bataan and Corregidor. The leadership of the ADBC found it difficult to believe the allegations of some activists about experimentation by Unit 731 doctors at Mukden because, they said, when they repeatedly asked at ADBC conventions for Mukden survivors to step forward and tell of their experiences in this regard, none did. And at its September 1986 hearing, the House Veterans Affairs Subcommittee on Compensation, Pensions and Insurance told witnesses who testified that the subcommittee needed documentary evidence, not just anecdotal data, before they could recommend special compensation or benefits for former Mukden POWs.[1]

It was not until May 1995, when a television crew from the Japanese network Nippon TV (NTV) came to the ADBC reunion in Braintree, Massachusetts, that some Mukden former POWs broke their silence. The Japanese television team was preparing a one-hour documentary on all the activities of Unit 731, and apparently some Mukden survivors were motivated to let the Japanese people know their stories, even if they had not been able or willing to discuss this matter with their families or fellow former POWs.

Former Pfc. Robert Brown and SSgt. Art Campbell gave extensive interviews to the Japanese producers, Shoji Kondo and Fuyuko Nishisato. Then Kondo and Nishisato traveled to Michigan, where they interviewed former Sgt. Herman Castillo at length. Castillo had never spoken of his nightmare confined in a cage to anyone before; his interviews with the Japanese TV crew and, later, with me are the only times before his 2005 death that he spoke about his ordeal. The Japanese documentary, broadcast nationwide in late 1995 in Japan, contains brief excerpts of their interview with Castillo, but the recollections of Art Campbell and medic Robert Brown were not included. Since the NTV documentary was only aired in Japan, American TV audiences did not see it—and only a small portion dealt with one Mukden survivor, Castillo.

Professor Sheldon Harris, in the 2002 updated edition of his landmark book on Unit 731, *Factories of Death*, devoted an entire chapter to exploring the question of whether the Mukden POWs were used for Unit 731 experimentation. At the end of the chapter on Mukden, published shortly before he died, Harris wrote, "The passage of time, the seeming negligence on the part of the Army in not providing the prisoners with exhaustive physical exams and detailed debriefings, and the paucity of available records make it almost impossible for the modern researcher to offer a definitive answer. . . . Although American POWs may have been the victims of BW tests, there is no substantive evidence currently available to prove that the experiments took place at Camp Mukden."[2] However, in a footnote to this chapter, Harris noted the formation of the Nazi War Crimes and Japanese Imperial Records Interagency Working Group (IWG), on which I served as a historical advisor during the IWG's seven years of work, and expressed his hope that "such evidence may be discovered in the future. . . . [The legislation creating the IWG] provided for the complete disclosure of Japanese Imperial Army wartime documents still housed in American archives."[3]

After Shoji Kondo correctly translated for me in June 2002 a key phrase, "the officer in charge of the Kwantung Army's Anti-Infection and Water Supply Main Depot," in the order (number 98) given by Commanding General Yoshijiro Umezu of the Kwantung Army and my subsequent discovery of that same key phrase in a Japanese defendant's Tokyo trial transcript, I presented the first corroborating documentation of Unit 731 activities at Mukden to the IWG in September 2002. Chapters 4, 5, and 6 of this book provide substantial additional data to illuminate the role of Unit 731 medical teams at the Mukden camp and the long-term consequences of their activities to some American survivors.

These pages represent the first time that a more complete accounting of Unit 731 visits to the Mukden camp has been presented in English. If the mystery of the scope—and limits—of Unit 731's involvement with some Mukden POWs has at last been clarified, other mysteries about this camp remain unsolved. Why didn't American investigators and medical personnel ask liberated Mukden POWs about visits by Japanese doctors from outside the camp? Why did some Mukden returnees feel isolated and even quarantined for a period of time? And why did some of them feel they were treated so differently from others returning from the Pacific?

Why did the Russians prevent the OSS's Col. J. F. Donovan from reaching Port Arthur to inquire about the whereabouts of SSgt. William Lynch? Was it because they knew Port Arthur was to become a Soviet naval base and that Donovan was an intelligence officer? Donovan perhaps did not know about the secret agreement reached by Premier Josef Stalin, President Franklin D. Roosevelt, and Prime Minister Winston Churchill until February 1947, when the agreement was finally made public. Are Lynch's remains buried in a field at Lushun near the former *Kempeitai* prison? If so, will they be located and finally returned, after sixty-five years, to his family in Boston? This latter mystery is perhaps the only one that may be resolved in the near future. The others will probably remain the subject of conjecture indefinitely.

Meanwhile the remaining survivors of Mukden share with their fellow former POWs of the Pacific war a lingering sadness about the way they have been treated in the postwar years. A common refrain is, "We fought the enemy, then came back to find we were fighting our own government." Between the red tape of dealing with an often-clueless series of VA doctors and the failed attempts to seek compensation for their unique suffering from Congress—not to mention the rebuffs from the Japanese government, its corporations, and our own State Department—it's easy for these patriotic veterans to feel disheartened.

Occasionally there is a ray of hope, such as the understanding expressed by Anthony Principi, the former secretary of veterans affairs, when he gave the keynote speech to members of the ADBC at their annual convention in Hampton, Virginia, in May 2001. "Being a prisoner of war is unlike anything else," Secretary Principi remarked. "In combat," he continued, "you engage the enemy, then withdraw to fight another day. But when you are a prisoner of war, the enemy surrounds you, every day and every night."[4] Several veterans in the room expressed surprise to hear from a VA official who "gets it" about the stress of daily captivity and the lasting effects of that stress. Between that stress and the medical experimentations we now know were carried out by Unit 731, for many survivors of Japanese captivity, the war has never completely ended.

Notes

Chapter 1. The Long Heartbreak Begins

1. Edward Jackfert and Andrew Miller, eds., *History of the Defenders of the Philippines* (Paducah, Ky.: Turner Publishing, 1991), 15.
2. Fireside chat, February 23, 1942, Fireside Chats, Franklin D. Roosevelt Presidential Library and Museum, Hyde Park, N.Y.
3. Dorothy Cave, *Beyond Courage: One Regiment Against Japan, 1941–1945* (Las Cruces, N.M.: Yucca Tree Press, 1992), 124–25.
4. As it was handwritten, Roosevelt's reply was not "official," and it is not in the archives at the Franklin D. Roosevelt Library in Hyde Park. The only known copy was in the files of the long-defunct Bataan Families Organization, Los Angeles chapter.
5. Jackfert and Miller, *History of the Defense of the Philippines*, 40.
6. Leo Padilla, interview with the author, Albuquerque, N.M., May 2003.
7. One of the first Japanese commanders tried for war crimes was General Masaharu Homma, who had command responsibility for Bataan. When asked at his 1946 trial in Manila why he did not provide food for the POWs during the long Death March, Homma blithely answered, "I thought they had their own food." He was hanged on February 23, 1946.
8. Figures compiled by the American Ex-Prisoners of War, Inc., Arlington, Tex., March 15, 2000.

Chapter 2. Voyage to a Frozen Hell and Deadly Camp

1. Sumio Adachi, *Unprepared Regrettable Events: A Brief History of Japanese Practices on Treatment of Allied War Victims During the Second World War* (Yokosuka: National Defense Academy of Japan, 1982), 14.
2. Gregory F. Michno, *Death on the Hellships* (Annapolis: Naval Institute Press, 2006), appendix.

3. Interviews with Sheldon Zimbler, quoted in his book *Undaunted Valor: Men of Mukden in Their Own Words* (Kingston, N.Y.: Tri-State, 2008), 205–8.

4. Gene Wooten to the author, May 2004.

5. John Zenda, interview with the author, April 10, 2009.

6. Oliver "Red" Allen, *Abandoned on Bataan: One Man's Story of Survival* (Boerne, Tex.: Crimson Horse, 2002), 105.

7. Ken Towery, *The Chow Dipper: A Personal and Political Odyssey* (Austin, Tex.: Eakin Press, 1994), 66.

8. Brown discovered postwar that it was the *Grenadier* that made the attack, and that the submarine's crew scuttled in 1943 and themselves became POWs. Zimbler, *Undaunted Valor*, 207.

9. Elmer Shabart, *Memoirs of a Barbed Wire Surgeon* (Oakland, Calif.: Regent Press, 1997), 41.

10. D. Randall Haley, *Once Forgotten: A World War Two Marine's Combat and Prisoner of War Story* (N.p.: privately published, 1994), 46.

11. Walter Middleton to the author, September 9, 2002.

12. Padilla interview.

13. Art Campbell, interviews with the author, Albuquerque, N.M., May 23–24, 2003.

14. Joseph A. Petak, *Never Plan Tomorrow* (Valencia, Calif.: Aquatur, 1991), 149.

15. Middleton to the author, September 9, 2002.

16. Document admitted for evidence only, International Military Tribunal of the Far East (IMTFE) (hereafter cited as trial of Colonel Genji Matsuda), transcript, pp. 14,503–5, RG 331, NARA (hereafter cited as RG 331, NARA).

17. Capt. Des Brennan, taped oral recollections, furnished to the author by Australian researcher Peter G. Winstanley.

18. Petak, *Never Plan Tomorrow*, 152 ff.

19. Gene Wooten to the author, June 1999.

20. Furyo Joho Kyuku, Summary of Treatment of POWs, published December 1955; and Collected Documents of National Legislation. Concerning POWs, published December 1946, cited repeatedly by Adachi, *Unprepared Regrettable Events*.

21. Petak, *Never Plan Tomorrow*, 152 ff.

22. Sgt. Charles Dragich, interview with the author, Albuquerque, N.M., May 24, 2003.

23. Ken Towery, remarks at the Admiral Nimitz National Museum of the Pacific War, Fredericksburg, Tex., March 16, 1995, and interview with the author, March 2, 2000.

24. Dragich interview.

25. Pvt. William "Dingle" Bell, taped oral memoir, sent to the author by Peter Winstanley, July 2002.

26. John Zenda, interview with the author, September 6, 2005.

27. Petak, *Never Plan Tomorrow*, 163.

28. Brennan taped oral recollections.

29. Leon Elliott to the author, July 2000.

30. Eddy Laursen, interview with the author, March 16, 2004.

31. Bell oral memoir.

32. Robert Brown, interview with the author, December 22, 2004.

33. Wooten to the author, June 1999.

34. Middleton to the author, September 9, 2002.

CHAPTER 3. MAN IN A CAGE: THE UNIT 731 DOCTORS COME TO MUKDEN

1. Defense Exhibit 3113, International Military Tribunal of the Far East (IMTFE) transcript, p. 27,814, Special Collections, Starr Law Library, Columbia University School of Law (hereafter cited as Starr Library).
2. Shoji Kondo, interview with the author, New York City, June 10, 2002.
3. Defense Document 2003, IMTFE transcript, pp. 27,814–15, Starr Library.
4. Diary of Maj. Robert Peaty, supplied privately to the author (hereafter cited as Peaty Diary).
5. Robert Brown, interview with the author, March 4, 2003.
6. Colonel Matsuda and the POW camp doctor, Captain Joichi Kuwashima, were tried in Shanghai on January 18, 1947. Their testimony will be discussed in a later chapter.
7. Fuyuko Nishisato, article in *Quarterly Report on Japan's War Responsibility*, Summer 1996. Translated for the author by Yuka Ibuki.
8. Ibid.
9. Herman Castillo, interviews with the author, May 8 and 10, 2003.
10. Lydia Castillo, interviews with the author, June 23 and 24, 2005, and April 30, 2009.
11. Letter of Maj. Stanley Hankins, IMTFE transcript, pp. 27,947–48, Starr Library.
12. Nishisato, article in *Quarterly Report*.
13. Peaty Diary, February 18, 1943, entry.
14. Walter Middleton, interview with the author, February 7, 2004.
15. Peaty Diary, February 8, 1943, entry.
16. True, these Japanese had trained at Tokyo Medical College, but they did not reveal that they were now working at Unit 731 in Ping Fan.
17. Robert Wolfersberger, interview with the author, March 11, 2004.
18. Paul Lankford, interview with the author, March 15, 2004.
19. David Levy, interview with the author, March 11, 2004.
20. William Wesley Davis, interview with the author, July 23, 1999.
21. Marie Bridges, letter to the author, June 15, 1999.
22. Robert Vogler, interview with the author, June 18, 2006.
23. This phrase has been interpreted by some researchers as having a sinister meaning (i.e., experimentation) but the "certain purpose" was in fact Mitsubishi's request for skilled white POW labor to be sent to the company's factory complex in Mukden.
24. Defense Document 2002, Defense Exhibit 3114, IMTFE, p. 27,817, Starr Library

CHAPTER 4. UNIT 731 DOCTORS CALL AGAIN AND AGAIN

1. Defense Doc. 22296-1, IMTFE transcript, p. 27,947, Tokyo War Crimes Trials, Starr Library.
2. Ibid.
3. Middleton interview, February 7, 2004.
4. Capt. William D. Thompson, "Narrative History—Mukden Group POW Allied Military Personnel at Jap Prisoners Camp, Mukden, Manchukuo," Entry 427, Box 1598, Records of the Adjutant General, Modern Military Records, RG 407, National Archives and Records Administration, College Park, Md. (NARA).
5. Testimony of Colonel Genji Matsuda, Shanghai, beginning January 18, 1947, Military Commission Convened by the Commanding General, United States

Forces, China Theater [Gen. Albert Wedemeyer], commencing February 28, 1946, Supreme Commander, Allied Forces, Pacific (SCAP), trial of Colonel Genji Matsuda, Stack 390, Box 1660, RG 331, NARA (hereafter cited as RG 331, NARA).

6. Peaty Diary, May 23, 1943, entry.

7. Campbell interviews.

8. Ibid.

9. Testimony of Lt. Col. Stanley Hankins, trial of Colonel Genji Matsuda, RG 331, NARA.

10. Ibid., 131, 142–43, 159.

11. "Materials on the Trial of Former Servicemen of the Japanese Army Charged with the Manufacture and Employing of Bacteriological Weapons," Foreign Language Publishing House, Moscow, 1950, Transcript 268. Provided to the author by Shoji Kondo.

12. Ibid., Separate Extract, Testimony of Tomio Karasawa, 9.

13. Russell Working, "The Trial of Unit 731," *Japan Times*, June 5, 2001.

CHAPTER 5. THE COLONEL'S RULES AND HIS "HOSPITAL"

1. Thompson, "Narrative History," 12.

2. Ibid., 13.

3. Ibid., 15.

4. Entry 460A, Box 2134, Records of the Provost Marshal General, American POW Information Bureau Records Branch, RG 389, NARA (hereafter cited as RG 389, NARA).

5. Affidavit of Elvin Davis, December 14, 1945, RG 389, NARA.

6. Affidavit of Victor Trask, January 11, 1946, RG 389, NARA.

7. Statement taken at the Mukden camp, September 15, 1945, from Richard Schroeder by the Judge Advocate General Office, War Department, Records of the Judge Advocate General, RG 153, NARA (hereafter cited as RG 153, NARA).

8. Affidavit of Earl Guye, December 21, 1945, RG 153, NARA

9. Affidavit of Theodore Mullikin, November 20, 1945, RG 153, NARA.

10. Affidavit of Eddy Laursen, December 1945, RG 153, NARA. Several ex-POWs from various Japanese camps have told this writer that the worst beatings they received were administered by nisei who had grown up in the United States and either volunteered or were tricked into returning to Japan. Many became camp interpreters; some, such as Lieutenant Murada, enlisted in the Imperial Japanese Army.

11. Affidavit of Albert Jones, January 11, 1946, RG 153, NARA.

12. Charges, trial of Colonel Genji Matsuda, RG 331, NARA.

13. "Report by Japs of Swiss Red Cross rep. of his inspection of this [Hoten] Camp," Entry 1357, Box 89, Records of the International Committee of the Red Cross, Records of the Department of State, RG 59, NARA (hereafter cited as Records of the Department of State, RG 59, NARA).

14. Marcel Junod, "I Found Wainwright in Prison Camp," *Coronet*, September 1952.

15. Diary of Capt. Des Brennan, M.D., December 3, 1942, entry.

16. Ibid., November 15, 19, and 27, 1942, entries.

17. See the full transcript of the trial of Colonel Genji Matsuda, RG 331, NARA.

18. Robert Brown, interviews with the author, March 2003–September 2007.

19. Testimony of Capt. Mark Herbst, trial of Colonel Genji Matsuda, RG 331, NARA.
20. Deposition of 1st Lt. Elmer Shabart, August 27, 1946, trial of Colonel Genji Matsuda, RG 331, NARA.
21. Thompson, "Narrative History," 63.
22. Ibid., 12.
23. Ibid., 23.
24. Brown interview, December 22, 2004.

Chapter 6. The MKK Factory: Daily Toil, Fear, and Sabotage

1. Li-Shiu Lee, statement at panel discussion at Shenyang, China, September 18, 2003.
2. Kondo interview.
3. Kenneth Kai, statement at panel talk at Shenyang, China, September 18, 2003.
4. Arthur Christie, *Mission Scapula* (UK: privately published, 2004), 105.
5. Affidavit by MKK president Tokujiro Kubota, August 5, 1947, used as Defense Exhibit 3127, trial of Colonel Genji Matsuda, RG 331, NARA.
6. Brennan taped oral recollections. Captain Brennan died in 2001.
7. Thompson, "Narrative History," 16. Captain Thompson was a lieutenant during captivity; he is referred to by that rank in this text. Note the discrepancy in spelling the full name of the MKK plant: I am using the most consistent spelling found in various narratives.
8. Robert Vogler and Herschel Bouchey, interviews with the author, Orlando, Fla., May 6, 2004.
9. Affidavits by Mukden ex-POWs, Entry 44, Box 306, Files 101–25, RG 153, NARA.
10. Affidavit of Richard Schroeder, September 15, 1945, Entry 44, Box 306, Files 101–25, RG 153, NARA.
11. Robert Wolfersberger to the author, August 2, 1999.
12. Affidavit of Charles Shelton, November 15, 1945, Entry 44, Box 306, Files 101–25, RG 153, NARA.
13. Affidavit of Raymond Adams, October 15, 1945, Entry 44, Box 306, Files 101–25, RG 153, NARA.
14. Affidavit of Bruce Callen, November 10, 1945, Entry 44, Box 306, Files 101–25, RG 153, NARA.
15. Affidavit of Arthur Wells, November 20, 1945, Oakland, Calif., Entry 44, Box 306, Files 101–25, RG 153, NARA.
16. Bell oral memoir.
17. Linda Goetz Holmes, *Unjust Enrichment: American POWs Under the Rising Sun*, 2nd ed. (Old Saybrook, Conn.: Konecky & Konecky, 2008), 29.
18. Thompson, "Narrative History," 25.
19. Vernon LaHeist to the author, August 1999.
20. Thompson, "Narrative History," 93
21. Robert O'Brien, news conference, New York, N.Y., September 14, 1999.
22. Affidavit of Tokujiro Kubota, August 5, 1947, IMTFE, Tokyo, Box 1660, RG 331, NARA.
23. Thompson, "Narrative History," 67.
24. Peaty Diary, October 13, 1944, entry.
25. Padilla interview.

26. Petak, *Never Plan Tomorrow*, 176–79.
27. Davis interview.
28. Herschel Bouchey, interview quoted in Stanwood, Wash., newspaper, December 3, 2008.
29. J. D. Beshears, interview with the author, San Antonio, Tex., May 29, 2009.
30. Bell oral memoir.
31. Philip Haley, interview with the author, March 5, 2004.
32. Randall Haley, article in *Ex-POW Bulletin*, January 2004.
33. Holmes, *Unjust Enrichment*, 87.

CHAPTER 7. MAJOR STANLEY HANKINS: A MAJOR MILITARY EMBARRASSMENT

1. Arnold Bocksel, interview with the author, April 19, 2005.
2. Campbell interviews.
3. Arnold Bocksel, interview with the author, March 6, 2004. In 1988 Bocksel was awarded the POW Medal of Honor, authorized by Congress in 1985. He has been honored many times by veterans' groups in Long Island, New York.
4. Herschel Bouchey, interview with the author, San Antonio, Tex., May 29, 2009.
5. J. D. Beshears, interview with the author, San Antonio, Tex., May 30, 2009.
6. Henry Harlan, interview with the author, March 6, 2004.
7. Zenda interview, September 6, 2005.
8. Eddy Laursen, interview with the author, March 6, 2004.
9. Robert Brown, interview with the author, March 5, 1999.
10. John Ward, statement about Bocksel to the Provost Marshal General's Office, RG 389, NARA.
11. Padilla interview.
12. Randall Edwards, interview with the author, San Antonio, Tex., May 29, 2009.
13. Testimony of Lt. Col. Stanley Hankins, 65.
14. Domei wire service story, July 20, 1943, Entry 427, Box 1598, RG 407, NARA.
15. Thompson, "Narrative History," 38.
16. Statement of Corporal Wantland, RG 389, NARA.
17. Statement of Harold Farrell, RG 389, NARA.
18. Affidavit of Thomas Proulx, October 10, 1945, RG 153, NARA.
19. Richard Boylan and William Cunliffe, researchers at NARA, interviews and communications with the author, May–June 2009.

CHAPTER 8. ESCAPE

1. Thompson, "Narrative History," 33.
2. Interview with historian Jing Yang, *Naval History*, February 2007, 34.
3. Decun Gao, comments at a panel discussion, Shenyang, China, September 18, 2003.
4. Affidavit of Thomas Bullock, October 1945, San Francisco, Entry 144, Box 306, Files 101–25, RG 153, NARA.
5. Affidavit of Thomas Proulx, October 29, 1945, Miami, Fla., Entry 144, Box 306, Files 101–25, RG 153, NARA.
6. Robert Wolfersberger, recollection, December 22, 1995, sent to the author August 2, 1997.

7. Thompson, "Narrative History," 39–40.
8. Excerpt of Colonel Genji Matsuda's report to Tokyo, used as an exhibit, trial of Colonel Genji Matsuda, RG 331, NARA.
9. Gao, comments at a panel discussion.
10. Detailed statement made by three recaptured POWs to *Kempeitai*, after prolonged beatings and torture, trial of Colonel Genji Matsuda, RG 331, NARA.
11. Thompson, "Narrative History," 42.
12. Edwards interview.
13. Thompson, "Narrative History," 43.
14. Interview with State Department official, *New York Times*, August 12, 1944, p. 7.
15. Testimony of Lieutenant Miki, trial of Colonel Genji Matsuda, RG 331, NARA.
16. Bocksel interview, April 19, 2005; Petak, *Never Plan Tomorrow*, 189.
17. Catherine Meringolo Quoma, interview with the author, January 26, 2005.
18. Julia Paliotto, statement to the Associated Press, July 31, 1944.
19. Patricia Paliotto Favulli to the author, July 21, 2009.
20. Jing Yang, slide presentation and talk given at Mukden Survivors reunion, Kingston, N.Y., September 8, 2005.

CHAPTER 9. RED CROSS DOUBLE-CROSSED

1. "Summary of Communications Between the Department of State and the Japanese Government, 18 Dec. 1941–24 Aug. 1945," communiqué from Secretary of State Cordell Hull to Japanese government, December 17, 1941, and reply from Japanese government, January 28, 1942, Records of the Department of State, RG 59, NARA.
2. Cablegram from International Committee of the Red Cross to Washington, D.C., quoting Japanese Prisoner of War Information Bureau, July 3, 1943, Records of the Department of State, RG 59, NARA.
3. Leslie G. Hall, *The Blue Haze: Incorporating the History of "A" Force Groups 3 & 5, Burma-Thai Railway, 1942–1943* (N.p.: privately published, 1985), 275.
4. Foreign Service Postings, telegram from Under Secretary of State Edward Stettinius to Swiss legation in Tokyo, February 11, 1944, RG 84, NARA.
5. Entry 9032 SZB 144610, Box 444, Declassified Records of the National Security Agency, RG 457, NARA.
6. Entry 9011, SRDJ 81496, Vice 9007, Declassified Records of the National Security Agency, RG 457, NARA.
7. Thompson, "Narrative History," 23.
8. Ibid., 32.
9. Peaty Diary, November 13, 1943, entry.
10. Thompson, "Narrative History," 48.
11. Report by ICRC representative Max Pestalozzi, December 15, 1943, Entry 1357, Box 89, Records of the Department of State, RG 59, NARA.
12. Thompson, "Narrative History," 50.
13. Diary of Leon Elliott, copy given to the author.
14. Thompson, "Narrative History," 58.
15. Diary of Leon Elliott, June 20–July 11, 1944, entries.
16. Arnold Bocksel, interview with the author, March 13, 2004.

17. Thompson, "Narrative History," 65.
18. Peaty Diary, August 22, 1944, entry.
19. Thompson, "Narrative History," 65.
20. Report of ICRC delegate Angst on visit to Mukden POW camp, December 1944, Records of the Department of State, RG 59, NARA.
21. Peaty Diary, December 7, 1944, entry.
22. Robert Brown, interview with the author, September 22, 2005.
23. Files on the Mukden POW camp, Entry 1357, Box 89, folder "Mukden '45," Records of the Department of State, RG 59, NARA.
24. Junod, "I Found Wainwright in Prison Camp."
25. Peaty Diary, August 6, 1945, entry.
26. Marcel Junod, *Warrior Without Weapons,* 2nd ed. (Geneva: International Committee of the Red Cross, 1982), 262.

Chapter 10. Another Escape: An Ongoing Mystery

1. The name in Spanish means "The Corrector." When the Philippine Islands were under Spanish rule, the government of Spain would once a year send El Corregidor to correct any administrative or legal errors the local government in Manila might have made during the previous year. A fortress was built for El Corregidor's residence on what is now Corregidor Island.
2. Roy Weaver, interview with the author, June 29, 2009.
3. Ibid.
4. Thompson, "Narrative History," 57
5. Col. J. F. Donovan, "Recovery and Evacuation of Allied Prisoners," report, Sec. II:20, Entry 360, Box 2437, Records of the Adjutant General, RG 407, NARA.
6. Ibid., Sec. II:22. Mukden medic Pfc. Robert Brown stated that Capt. Mark Herbst had also searched for Staff Sergeant Lynch, traveling to Harbin to see if by any chance he had been taken there, but this information cannot be confirmed because Herbst told his son before his death that he had discarded all his Mukden records.
7. Letter from collection of Lynch family, reproduced in *Dorchester (Mass.) Reporter,* December 11, 2008, 4.
8. Donovan, "Recovery and Evacuation."

Chapter 11. B-29s Bring Death, Hope, and Rescue

1. Bell oral memoir.
2. Ibid.
3. Zenda interview, September 6, 2005.
4. Petak, *Never Plan Tomorrow,* 288–94.
5. Thompson, "Narrative History," 71.
6. Brown interview, March 4, 2003.
7. Robert Brown, interview with the author, March 16, 2004.
8. Letter from the files of Robert A. Brown, commendation from the POW camp commander, Colonel Genji Matsuda, sent to the author.
9. Letter from the files of Robert Brown, commendation from the War Department, sent to the author.
10. Brown interview, March 16, 2004.

11. Brennan taped oral recollections.
12. Intercepted Japanese diplomatic message, Entry 9011, Declassified Records of the National Security Agency, RG 457, NARA.
13. Thompson, "Narrative History," 73.
14. Petak, *Never Plan Tomorrow*, 362.
15. For a detailed description of this directive and a display of the document, see Holmes, *Unjust Enrichment*, chap. 12.
16. Declassified Records of the National Security Agency, RG 457, NARA.
17. In exchange for distracting the Japanese on a new front, FDR and Churchill secretly promised Stalin South Sakhalin and the Kurile Islands, return of Port Arthur as a Soviet naval base, and an occupation zone in Korea.
18. Excerpts from Hal Leith, *POWs of Japanese Rescued!* (N.p.: privately published, 2003),16–17.
19. Affidavit of John Guidos, September 1, 1945, Mukden, RG 153, NARA.
20. Petak, *Never Plan Tomorrow*, 384–87.
21. Thompson, "Narrative History," 85.
22. Ibid., 90
23. Comment by United Press reporter Frank Tremaine at a symposium at the Admiral Nimitz National Museum of the Pacific War, Fredericksburg, Tex., March 19, 1995.

CHAPTER 12. THE LONG ROAD BACK

1. Reply to Ambassador Harriman, Entry 1357, Box 89, folder "Mukden '45," Records of the Department of State, RG 59, NARA.
2. Ibid.
3. Donovan, "Recovery and Evacuation."
4. Ibid.
5. Ibid.
6. Ibid.
7. Ibid.
8. Ibid.
9. MSgt. Fred. W. Friendly, article in *CBI Roundup*, October 1945. Supplied from his personal scrapbook to the author by Ruth Friendly, June 2009.
10. Anecdote related to the author by Ruth Friendly, June 15, 2009.
11. Fred W. Friendly, *Due to Circumstances Beyond Our Control* . . . (New York: Vintage Books, 1968), xvii.
12. See Holmes, *Unjust Enrichment*, 145–46.
13. Haley interview.
14. Robert Rosendahl, interview with the author, Shenyang, China, September 18, 2003.
15. Joseph Vater, interview with the author, February 7, 2004. The Vater photo collection can be viewed at the Brooke County Library in Wellsburg, West Virginia.
16. Hal Leith, interview with the author, September 10, 2005.
17. Trial of Colonel Genji Matsuda and Captain Joichi Kuwashima, RG 331, NARA.
18. Narrative of Mukden survivors coming aboard the hospital ship *Relief*, RG 389, NARA. Unfortunately the author of this narrative is not identified.
19. Hilary S. King, unpublished poems. Used with permission of the poet.

20. Art and Frances Campbell, interview with the author, Albuquerque, N.M., May 23, 2003.
21. Towery, *Chow Dipper*, 123.
22. Ibid.
23. Walter Middleton, interview with the author, Fontana, N.C., August 25, 2002.
24. Middleton to the author, September 9, 2002.
25. Walter Middleton, interview with the author, March 20, 2004.
26. Brown interview, March 16, 2004.
27. Joseph Astarita, interview with the author, November 12, 1998.

CHAPTER 13. JUSTICE IN THE AFTERMATH?

1. *New York Times*, interview with Joseph Keenan, June 18, 1946.
2. Research shared with the author in Kondo interview. Kondo interviewed the truck driver who transported two truckloads of General Ishii's documents from a shrine at Ishikawa in Kanagawa prefecture to the Ishii estate at night, where the documents were buried in a garden.
3. Tomorado Masada, interview with investigator Murray Sanders, Office of Naval Intelligence, Entry 199, Box 103, Folder CD 23, File 3, RG 330, NARA.
4. Ibid.
5. Figure compiled by the American Prisoner of War Association, Arlington, Tex., released March 2000. The figure includes not only members of the armed forces captured in the Philippines and elsewhere, but also civilians captured on Wake Island, Guam, and elsewhere, as well as merchant mariners captured at sea, all of whom were sent to military prison camps.
6. Directive of Japanese military, August 20, 1945, intercepted by Allied intelligence, SCAP, IMTFE, Entry 865, Exhibit 2011, International Prosecution Section, RG 331, NARA.
7. Robert Donihi, interview with the author, August 4, 2000.
8. Testimony of Sgt. Harry Simmons at trial of Eichi Noda, SCAP, Entry 1865, Box 9580, File 235, RG 331, NARA (hereafter cited as File 235, RG 331, NARA).
9. Ibid.
10. Testimony of Christopher Vissaris, File 235, RG 331, NARA.
11. Testimony of James Baldassare, File 235, RG 331, NARA.
12. Testimony of George Johnston, File 235, RG 331, NARA.
13. Testimony of Carl Doning, File 235, RG 331, NARA.
14. Herbert Bix, *Hirohito and the Making of Modern Japan* (New York: HarperCollins, 2000), 627–34, 651ff.
15. Trial of Colonel Genji Matsuda and Captain Joichi Kuwashima, RG 331, NARA.
16. David Casey to the author, February 12, 2008.
17. A total of 13,996 American civilians were interned by the Japanese in World War II; 1,536 died in captivity. A total of 23,000 civilian Dutch men, women, and children died in Japanese internment camps. Figures compiled by American Ex-Prisoners of War Association, Arlington, Tex., March 15, 2000.
18. Thomas Foley, reply to the author at a panel Q&A at symposium commemorating the fiftieth anniversary of the signing of the Treaty of Peace with Japan, September 7, 2001, San Francisco.

CHAPTER 14. BACK IN TIME

1. Neil Gagliano to the author, August 20, 2003.
2. Xinhuanet, official Chinese news service, October 8, 2003.
3. John Zenda, statement at press conference, New York City, May 26, 2006.

EPILOGUE

1. House Veterans Affairs Committee, Subcommittee on Compensation, Pensions and Insurance Hearing, 88th Cong., September 17, 1986, *Congressional Record*, September 17, 1986.
2. Sheldon Harris, *Factories of Death: Japanese Biological Warfare, 1932–1945, and the American Cover-up*, rev. ed. (New York: Routledge, 2002), 167, 171.
3. Ibid.; see footnote 107 on page 176.
4. Anthony Principi, keynote speech, ADBC Convention, Hampton, Va., May 19, 2001.

Bibliography

BOOKS

Allen, Oliver. *Abandoned On Bataan: One Man's Story of Survival*. Boerne, Tex.: Crimson Horse, 2002.

Bix, Herbert P. *Hirohito and the Making of Modern Japan*. New York: HarperCollins, 2000.

Brackman, Arnold. *The Other Nuremberg*. New York: William Morrow, 1987.

Cave, Dorothy. *Beyond Courage: One Regiment Against Japan, 1941–45*. Las Cruces, N.M.: Yucca Tree Press, 1992.

Christie, Arthur. *Mission Scapula*. UK: privately published, 2004.

Friendly, Fred W. *Due to Circumstances Beyond Our Control . . .* New York: Vintage Books, 1968.

Haley, Randall. *Once Forgotten: A World War Two Marine's Combat and Prisoner of War Story*. N.p.: privately published, 1994.

Hall, Leslie G. *The Blue Haze: Incorporating the History of "A" Force Groups 3 & 5, Burma-Thai Railway, 1942–43*. N.p.: privately published, 1985.

Harris, Sheldon H. *Factories of Death: Japanese Biological Warfare, 1942–45 and the American Cover-Up*. Rev. ed. New York: Routledge, 2002.

Holmes, Linda Goetz. *Unjust Enrichment: American POWs Under the Rising Sun*. Rev. ed. Old Saybrook, Conn.: Konecky & Konecky, 2008.

Junod, Marcel. *Warrior Without Weapons*. 2nd ed. Geneva: International Committee of the Red Cross, 1982.

Kondo, Shoji. *Evidence of Unit 731 Crimes*. Harbin, Manchuria: Heilongjiang, 2001.

Leith, Hal. *POWs of Japanese Rescued!* N.p.: privately published, 2003.

Petak, Joseph A. *Never Plan Tomorrow*. Valencia, Calif.: Aquatur, 1991.

Shabart, Elmer. *Memoirs of a Barbed Wire Surgeon*. Oakland, Calif.: Regent Press, 1997.

Towery, Ken. *The Chow Dipper: A Personal and Political Odyssey*. Austin, Tex.: Eakin Press, 1994.

Worthington, Josiah W. *Hell and Beyond: A Diary of War and Captivity.* Edited by
   Frances W. Lipe. N.p.: privately published, 2006.
Zimbler, Sheldon. *Undaunted Valor: Men of Mukden in Their Own Words.* Kingston, N.Y.:
   Tri-State, 2008.

ARCHIVES

Foreign Language Publishing House, Moscow
   "Materials on the Trial of Foreign Servicemen of the Japanese Army Charged
   with the Manufacture and Employing of Biological Weapons." Transcript 268.
   Excerpts. 1950.
Franklin D. Roosevelt Presidential Library and Museum, Hyde Park, N.Y.
   Fireside Chats
MacArthur Memorial Library, Norfolk, Va.
   Papers of the Southwest Pacific Area, RG 3
   War Crimes Messages Collection, RG 9
Modern Military Records, National Archives and Records Administration, College
   Park, Md.
   Declassified Records of the National Security Agency, RG 457
   International Military Tribunal of the Far East (IMTFE), RG 331
   Records of the Adjutant General, RG 407
   Records of the Department of State, RG 59
   Records of the Judge Advocate General, RG 153
   Records of the Provost Marshal General, RG 389
Special Collections, Starr Law Library, Columbia University School of Law, New York,
   N.Y.

DIARIES

Diary of Capt. Des Brennan, M.D.. Collection of the author.
Diary of Leon Elliott. Collection of the author.
Diary of Maj. Robert Peaty. Collection of the author (copy at NA).

Index

About the Author

Linda Goetz Holmes is a recognized expert in the history of American POWs in the Pacific theater during World War II. She is the author of *Unjust Enrichment: How Japan's Companies Built Postwar Fortunes Using American POWs* and *4000 Bowls of Rice: A Prisoner of War Comes Home.*